CW00322194

Ian & Hazel Hutchinson
Casement Cottage
Ashford
Co. Wicklow
Tel. 0404-40251

Golden Retrievers

Ch. Styal Scott of Glengilde, the breed's record-holder, with 42 CCs. He is the sire of six champions. (Photo Dalton)

GOLDEN RETRIEVERS

AN OWNER'S COMPANION

Lyn Anderson

The Crowood Press

First published in 1991 by
The Crowood Press Ltd
Ramsbury, Marlborough
Wiltshire SN8 2HR

This impression 1993

British Library Cataloguing-in-Publication Data

Anderson, Lyn
  Golden retrievers.
  1. Dogs
  I. Title
  636.752

ISBN 1 85223 609 4

Cover photographs
front: Sh.Ch. Linchael Cartier of Gloi.
back: Sh.Ch. Linchael Cartier of Gloi (top left), with Sh.Ch.
Linchael Freya (top right); Sh.Ch. Linchael Persian Orchid
(bottom left), with Linchael Gullviva (bottom right).

Line-drawings by Annette Findlay.

Dedication
To Show Champion Linchael Delmoss, who made it
all possible.

Printed in Great Britain by Redwood Press Ltd,
Melksham, Wilts.

Contents

Acknowledgements

My sincere thanks to all those who have contributed photographs. I am indebted to Dr Larry Roberts, MRCVS for his excellent chapter on Ailments and Diseases, and to Joyce Hays, who not only typed the manuscript but had to decipher my illegible handwriting first.

1

History of the Breed

Guisachan House, in Invernesshire has become a place of pilgrimage for devotees of the Golden Retriever. Early in the 1850s, Sir Dudley Coutts Marjoribanks (who in 1866 became Lord Tweedmouth) was a guest at the house, and so great was his liking for the place that in 1854, he purchased the house from the Frasers for £52,000.

Our interest in Lord Tweedmouth lies with Golden Retrievers, but an Inverness farmers' year book shows he was highly regarded as a breeder of pure-bred Highland and Aberdeen Angus Cattle. He also bred ponies and is known, through the records of his daughter, to have kept Pointers, Deerhounds and Cairn Terriers.

Guisachan House.

For many years, a rather romantic theory regarding the origins of the Golden Retriever was accepted. This concerned a troupe of circus dogs and makes good, if inaccurate, reading.

In 1914, an article appeared in *Country Life* magazine entitled 'The Russian or Yellow Retriever' in which Arthur Croxton-Smith went into great detail regarding the theory of the circus dogs. Elma Stonex later disproved this theory after many years of extensive research. There are, however, inhabitants of the area surrounding the Guisachan Estate who are convinced the romantic story is true. True or not, it is worth recounting.

Croxton-Smith tells how the first Lord Tweedmouth was impressed by a group of circus dogs in Brighton and bought them. Dogs from this Russian breed were given to friends and acquaintances. The Right Hon. Lewis Harcourt M.P. exhibited his specimens of this breed as Golden Retrievers at several shows.

It is interesting to note that Duncan MacLennan (who followed in his father and grandfather's footsteps as headkeeper on the Guisachan Estate) states that his mother possessed a photograph of a group of dogs bought by the first Lord Tweedmouth between 1860 and 1870 from a party of Russians who were performing with them in Brighton. One would imagine that a family so entrenched in family history would be unlikely to make many mistakes about the livestock in their care.

Mrs Charlesworth, founder of the Golden Retriever Club, tells us that the Russian Retrievers acquired by Lord Tweedmouth were pale biscuit, cream or sometimes nearly white, with long wavy coats and the usual 'snow' dog's curly tail.

Lord Tweedmouth is believed to have introduced Bloodhound into his breeding programme. This resulted in colours which ranged from very pale biscuit through to tan. It also resulted in brown or pink noses, which were considered very ugly.

At the time Croxton-Smith was writing, he mentioned Colonel the Hon. W. le Poer Trench, who was exhibiting dogs of the same type under the title of Russian or Yellow Retrievers. He states: 'These, as a careful investigation of their antecedents proves, are descendants of the unadulterated Russian dogs acquired by Mr Marjoribanks in the fifties'.

Among the dogs exhibited by Colonel Trench were St. Hubert's Duke, St. Hubert's Czar, St. Hubert's Prince, St. Hubert's Paul, St. Hubert's Vesta and St. Hubert's May. Judging from the photographs, Vesta looks quite dateless in type and it is easy to imagine

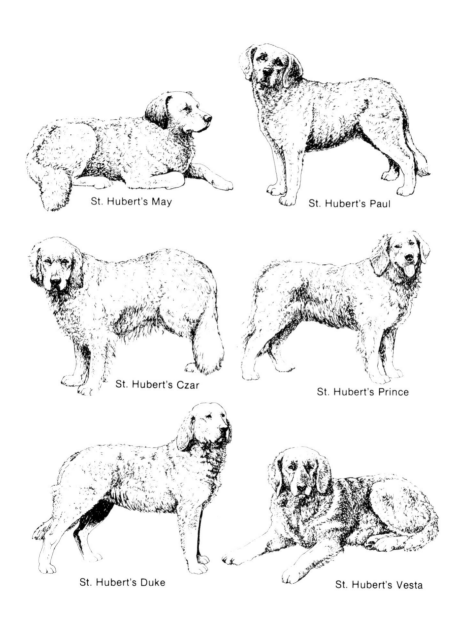

St. Hubert's May

St. Hubert's Paul

St. Hubert's Czar

St. Hubert's Prince

St. Hubert's Duke

St. Hubert's Vesta

Colonel le Poer Trench's Golden Retrievers.

walking into the ring with her today and that she would hold her own. It is interesting to observe how much like a Chesapeake Bay Retriever was St. Hubert's Duke.

St. Hubert's May is an intriguing one, because under her photograph the caption states: 'The Albino'. We are told that the Colonel was reluctant to breed from May in case her light eyes, pink nose and lips should become obvious in her progeny. She did, however, produce twenty-seven puppies in her lifetime and, as far as one may ascertain from black and white photographs, all were well pigmented.

Croxton-Smith relates how Colonel le Poer Trench was walking a dog bred by Lord Chichester when he met Lord Tweedmouth. The latter exclaimed how much this dog resembled the original Russian Retrievers. However, the Sixth Lord Chichester believes it unlikely that these two ever met.

We are also told that Colonel Trench met a German travelling on the London Underground. The Colonel had with him a yellow retriever and the German said he was once in the Caucasus and had met six fierce dogs, which were identical to the Colonel's own. They were kept to guard flocks from wolves and bandits. The Colonel is supposed to have sent someone to purchase two puppies, on his behalf, but unfortunately these were eaten by wolves on their journey down the mountains.

It is interesting to note that Croxton-Smith, who put forward these ideas of the origins of the breed was to doubt them later. Thirteen years after the article in *Country Life* was published, he stated that he had been told by Lord Tweedmouth's grandson that his grandfather obtained his first yellow dog from a Brighton cobbler and that it was the only yellow puppy in a litter of black wavy-coated retrievers.

In 1952, the Sixth Earl of Chichester (Lord Tweedmouth's great nephew) wrote an article in *Country Life*, entitled 'The Origin of the Yellow Retriever'. In this article he declared that it had been his intention for some time to state the history of the breed from his early recollections.

When the Guisachan Estate was sold in 1906, Lord Harcourt (who already had one puppy and possibly more) was given a number of dogs which remained in the kennels. These dogs were shown and the name Golden Retriever was used.

The Earl of Chichester states that one irrefutable piece of evidence exists in the stud book kept by Sir Dudley Marjoribanks from 1835.

In this he recorded the names and pedigrees of his Pointers, hounds and spaniels. Beagles are also recorded. A retriever is mentioned in 1842 and then another in 1857. This book records the names of retrievers and their breeding but does not give their colour. Lady Pentland had this most valuable of records in her possession but it is now housed at the Kennel Club.

The Russian story is questionable in the light of information given by the Earl of Chichester. He states that the year the dogs were purchased from the circus troupe was supposedly 1868 and one of these dogs was Nous. Yet an entry in the stud book for Nous is dated some four years earlier and describes him as 'Lord Chichester's breed. June 1864'.

The Earl of Chichester continues by saying that although he never had any faith in the Russian theory, one entry in the book made him reconsider. The name Sancho, dated April 1868, appears at the bottom of that year's list. It is a possible circus name and would account for the affirmation that a Russian dog did arrive at Guisachan.

From the stud book, a few more facts may be gleaned: 'Tweed, Ladykirk Breed, 1863' was given to Sir Dudley Marjoribanks by a relative, David Robertson M.P., who had changed his name from Marjoribanks. Tweed died in 1867 and David Robertson replaced him with Belle, shown as '1863 Ladykirk breed'.

Nous and Belle were mated and the result was four yellow puppies, born in June 1868. As we have a reasonably complete pedigree for this litter, it is of great interest to students of the breed. Lord Tweedmouth retained two of this litter, Cowslip and Primrose. His son, Edward Marjoribanks, was given Crocus and the Fifth Earl of Chichester accepted Ada as the foundation of the Chichester line of Golden Retrievers.

In the record book, written in Lord Tweedmouth's handwriting, Crocus, Belle, Primrose and Ada are named as 'Tweed Water-Spaniels'. All attempts have failed at positively identifying this breed over the years. Several photographs and paintings exist of these four bitches and they certainly look like the Golden Retriever as we know it.

Ada has been immortalized on canvas by Graves (1875) and by Goddard (1873). In the Graves painting, Ada is shown as a seven year old of relatively short coat. Her head is well proportioned although the ears are somewhat houndy and pendulous. She is shown with her front paws on the knee of the Fifth Earl of Chichester. In the painting

Danesdyke Dyna, the foundation bitch of the Boltby Kennel at 12 years old.

by Goddard, she is very much the type of Golden we are familiar with now. She has a good reach of neck and is deep in the brisket. The quarters appear well muscled and she has good feet. There seems to be very little similarity between Ada and her sire Nous, but even less between her and the St. Hubert's dogs, which were much more massive and had heavier heads. Whether we are able to see any family likeness or not is irrelevant as they must have been descended from her.

The Sixth Earl of Chichester states that another dog bearing the name Tweed was given to Lord Tweedmouth in 1872. Tweed was mated to Cowslip in 1873 and Topsy was the result. Brass (out of the Fifth Earl of Chichester's Ada) was sent to live with a keeper in 1874. Crocus reverted to Lord Tweedmouth's ownership and, when mated to Zoe (by Sambo, ex Topsy) in 1881 produced three yellow puppies. It is noted that black dogs mated to yellow bitches nearly always resulted in yellow litters.

As the dogs at Guisachan were also used for tracking, it is not surprising that a dog of half Bloodhound breeding was used to improve their ability in this area. There is also a note stating that a Bloodhound of sandy colouring was used.

*Mrs Charlesworth in 1934
with Ch. Noranby Diana,
Ch. Noranby Dutiful and
Ch. Noranby Deirdre.*

It is regrettable that no record of the Ilchester matings was kept. We know (from the Sixth Earl) that dogs with black, wavy coats were used and also black Labradors. It is known that a black dog called Sweep sired several litters and that he was most likely the sire of Robin (featured in Van der Weyde's painting, around 1880). Robin appears to be rather hard in expression and short in the muzzle but he is undeniably a Golden Retriever. The sixth Earl tells us that 'the picture of him does not do him justice'. He also says he was '. . . a first-class worker with a beautiful nose and mouth and a splendid water dog'.

There is a considerable gap after Robin but at the end of the 1890s an out-cross bitch was given to the fifth Earl. She was small and dark coloured, but few puppies were produced and eventually the strain came to an end.

Lord Tweedmouth gave some of his dogs to friends and the Ingestre kennel of the Earl of Shrewsbury was started with these lines. The Culham kennel was founded by Viscount Harcourt on stock bred by the Earl of Portsmouth. In 1908, dogs bearing the Culham prefix were shown at Cruft's and Crystal Palace.

So where did the breed progress from here? It was Mrs Charlesworth who worked so untiringly for the breed over the next few years. She acquired a bitch without a pedigree and named her Normanby Beauty. (This is slightly confusing as Mrs Charlesworth's prefix was Noranby.) Normanby Beauty was mated to Culham Brass and, in 1908, Noranby Balfour was born. In 1912, Noranby Campfire was born and he has a place in history as the first Golden Retriever to be a champion on the bench.

The breed's popularity on the bench made slow progress. In 1909, there were eight Golden Retrievers shown at Cruft's and two more appeared the following year. It should be remembered that there was no separate classification for them at shows at this time.

The year 1913 is of enormous importance to the breed, as it was then that Mrs Charlesworth founded the Golden Retriever Club, which formulated the first ever Standard for the Breed. In the same year, the Kennel Club classified the breed as separate from the other retrievers, under the title of 'Golden or Yellow Retrievers'.

Mrs Harrison with Boltby Skylon (later Ch.) winning his first CC in the late 1950s. Also shown is Jean Brison (later Mrs Burnett) and Ch. Fordvale Gay Moon Lynne. (Photo Cooke)

In 1920, the first ever dual champion appeared. This was Mr R. Hermon's Ch. and F.T. Ch. Balcombe Boy (by Culham Tip, ex Culham Amber II). He was bred by Lord Harcourt and presented to Mr Herman. He was just two years old when he attained both titles. It would be enough to remember him as the first dual champion for the breed but his influence on the breed was enormous. When mated to Balcombe Bunty (by Ottershaw Brilliant, ex Syrup), Ch. Haulstone Dan resulted, as did Haulstone Rusty who was great grandam of Ch. Colthill Dan and Gilder.

When Ch. Balcombe Boy was mated to Noranby Daybreak (by Ch. Noranby Campfire, ex Dandelion), amongst the winning progeny was Ch. Noranby Daydawn, through whom are descended many champions.

From 1900 onwards, so many kennels were started that a book devoted to them would be needed to record their breeding programmes and successes in the field.

As Guisachan House is the nearest to a monument that exists for our breed, it is interesting to know what eventually happened to the estate. When Lord Tweedmouth died in 1894, and his widow eleven years later, a fountain and trough were erected to their memory on the outskirts of Tomich village.

Ch. Lakol of Yelme (left) with her two sons, Ch. Bard of Cleavers and Ch. Nicodemus of Cleavers.

Lord Tweedmouth's son Edward inherited the house, but left in 1904, on the death of his wife. His job as First Lord of the Admiralty took most of his time, leaving little to be spent at Guisachan. Poor health and increasing financial worries led to the sale of Guisachan in 1908. The estate was sold but Tomich House (now Tomich Hotel) was kept for use as a shooting lodge.

Edward's son Dudley Churchill Marjoribanks became the third Lord Tweedmouth on his father's death in 1909. There were no male heirs from his marriage to Viscount Middleton's daughter Muriel, and so the Tweedmouth title became extinct.

Lord Portsmouth bought the estate and used it as a shooting lodge. Few changes were made to the estate and on 16th June 1919 it was put up for auction in Hanover Square, London. There was not a single buyer.

It was not until 1935 that the estate was sold, this time to Lady Aberdeen's lawyer, Mr Hunter. The following year, attempts were made to sell the houses in Tomich, the most expensive being advertised at £65, but only a few were sold.

There was an asking price of £3,500 for Guisachan House, including its 150 acres of parkland, but there were no buyers. Lady Aberdeen rented it to the National Fitness Campaign's committee as a training estate.

The approach of war interrupted any future plans which Lady Aberdeen had for Guisachan and, in 1939, Lady Islington, who lived nearby, became increasingly disenchanted with the activities of the Fitness movement. She purchased the house for £1,500 and first removed the roof. The elements have done the rest of the demolition work during the intervening years.

Mr Michael Waddel bought the home farm and a small area surrounding it. The Forestry Commission acquired a larger area and the largest area of all was sold as sporting estates. When Mr Waddel died in 1960, the estate was bought by Euan Fraser, returning the house to the possession of the Fraser family. Six years later, the estate was sold, yet again, to Colonel James Fraser, and now belongs to Donald, his younger son.

I visited the estate again this summer and I found the obvious decay, which had taken place over the five years since I was last there, quite distressing. It was once a very grand house in a very beautiful setting. There was something very sad about seeing the only tangible link with the ancestry of our breed almost in ruin. How lovely if a permanent memorial could be erected on the site.

2

Pedigree

Ask the average dog owner about his pure-bred dog and he will inform you that it possesses a pedigree 'as long as your arm'. But it is the content of the pedigree that matters, not its length. Indeed, pedigrees come in three-, four- and five-generation lengths. The length of a dog's pedigree has no bearing on the quality of the animal.

When I began breeding Golden Retrievers, I was amazed to find that I was entrusted with the important task of providing each puppy with a pedigree. At first glance, the task seemed daunting but it is remarkably easy, if incredibly painstaking. The top half of a puppy's pedigree is a straight copy of the sire's pedigree. The bottom half is a copy of the dam's pedigree. As each generation is given a pedigree, so the final line of names disappears to make room for the addition of the new sire and dam at the front.

The way in which you write out a pedigree for each of your puppies is a matter of personal choice, but it has become a tradition to record champions, show champions, field-trial champions and obedience champions in red ink. Some breeders write the actual names in red, others underline the names in red.

A typed pedigree looks immaculate but, for me, lacks something of the character of a handwritten one. Some of the very early pedigrees from around the 1940s have added interest for me because they were handwritten by the breeder. Many of the pedigrees in my possession are signed by breeders long since dead and it is a strange feeling to read their signatures alongside the dates. Some of these documents are executed in the most beautiful copperplate style and would have gained nothing from being typed.

If your handwriting borders on the illegible, it is a good idea to write in capital letters. Check the spelling of the names you are writing. It is amazing how many pedigrees contain not only minor mis-spellings but whole words which are incorrect. It is not hard to imagine how a novice breeder might interpret the handwritten 'Nordic Ch. Mjaerumhogda's Crusader', or 'Mjaerumhogda's Thyra to Standfast at Linchael'! It is a humbling thought that the document you are presently compiling could exist years after your death. Any inaccuracies on your part could be replicated many times in the future.

For a fee, the Kennel Club can provide you with a computerized pedigree of your dog. It looks very attractive and is accurate. It is worth mentioning that the Kennel Club also offers other computerized records. For instance, you may apply for a record of your dog's Championship Show wins, which is particularly useful if you buy an adult or if you sell an adult abroad. Other services offered by the Kennel Club include a record of your bitch's progeny, your stud-dog's record and a list of the Challenge Certificates awarded by a particular judge.

To the novice, the pedigree is a collection of unfamiliar and, frequently, unpronounceable names. But, as you become more familiar with the canine world, you will start to construct a mental picture of the dogs named in the pedigree and be able to recall the attributes of these dogs.

Many will have been shown before you participated in the sport, but old club yearbooks are an excellent source of photographic information. For instance, you can start to work out where your dog's good (or bad) shoulders came from. You can also see why your dog lacks coat or possesses it in profusion.

During the last few years, breeders have started to add information to pedigrees which is of enormous value. It has become the norm to include the dog's hip score (*see* page 185), so this will appear as, for example, 2:4 beneath the registered name. It is also usual to include the date of the most recent eye certificate and this will appear as 'certificate of freedom from progressive retinal atrophy (PRA) and HC', followed by the date. Be absolutely accurate when you record your dog's hip-score and eye clearance as it is an offence to make a false claim. Any incorrect information may result in unexpected problems for years to come, so your role as an honest, accurate recorder is of the utmost importance.

The dogs featured on your dog's pedigree may be visually different from one another, but they have one over-riding common factor: they are all representatives of the Breed Standard, which states how a Golden Retriever should look. Over the years it has been revised but the basics remain. The Kennel Club owns the copyright of the Breed Standards for this country. The American Standard is similar to the British one but it is more detailed.

PEDIGREE

The UK Breed Standard

(Reproduced by kind permission of the Kennel Club of Great Britain)

General Appearance

Symmetrical, balanced, active, powerful, level mover; sound with kindly expression.

Characteristics

Biddable, intelligent and possessing natural working ability.

Temperament

Kindly, friendly and confident.

Head and Skull

Balanced and well chiselled, skull broad without coarseness; well set on neck, muzzle powerful, wide and deep. Length of foreface approximately equals length from well-defined stop to occiput. Nose preferably black.

Eyes

Dark brown, set well apart, dark rim.

Ears

Moderate size, set on approximate level with eyes.

Mouth

Jaws strong, with a perfect, regular and complete scissor bite, i.e. upper teeth closely overlapping lower teeth and set square to the jaws.

Neck

Good length, clean and muscular.

Forequarters

Forelegs straight with good bone, shoulders well laid back, long in blade with upper arm of equal length placing legs well under body. Elbows close fitting.

Body

Balanced, short coupled, deep through heart. Ribs deep, well sprung. Level topline.

Hindquarters

Loin and legs strong and muscular, good second thighs, well-bent stifles. Hocks well let down, straight when viewed from rear, neither turning in nor out. Cowhocks highly undesirable.

Feet

Round and cat-like.

Tail

Set on and carried level with back, reaching to hocks without curl at tip.

Gait/Movement

Powerful with good drive. Straight and true in front and rear. Stride long and free with no sign of hackney action in front.

Coat

Flat or wavy with good feathering, dense water-resisting undercoat.

Colour

Any shade of gold or cream, neither red nor mahogany. A few white hairs on chest only, permissible.

Size

Height at withers: Dogs 56–61cm (22–24in); Bitches 51–56cm (20–22in).

Faults

Any departure from the foregoing points should be considered a fault and the seriousness with which the fault should be regarded should be in exact proportion to its degree.

Note Male animals should have two apparently normal testicles fully descended into the scrotum.

It is interesting to ask a group of people to read this Standard and then to question them on their interpretation. Each will have a slightly different picture of what is written. We are, after all, relying on the printed word for a visual image, and since we each perceive things differently, one person's 'kindly expression' may be someone else's 'hard expression'. There are, however, parts of the Standard which are pure fact and not open to individual interpretation. An example of this is the ideal shoulder construction, which states, 'long in the blade with upper arm of equal length, placing legs well under body'.

The Golden Retriever described in the Breed Standard is the ideal for the breed but, in reality, it does not exist. Think of the most perfectly constructed dog you know and he will always deviate from the Standard. This deviation might be almost imperceptible, but it is there. To produce a Golden Retriever that brings the Breed Standard to life is what every breeder aims for. The nearer one gets, the more absorbing the quest for perfection becomes.

If the Standard is to be our blueprint for success, it is important that we should analyse it and, by this analysis, come to understand it more fully.

Interpreting the Breed Standard

General Appearance

The Golden Retriever is essentially a working gundog, so his construction must fit him for the job he was intended to do. He may

Ch. Styal Stephanie of Camrose, aged 10 years, the breed's record-holding bitch. She is the epitome of balance. (Photo Pearce)

need to work over frozen, ploughed fields carrying a large bird of considerable weight. A lightly built, short-necked and low-legged dog would obviously be ill-equipped for such a task.

The balanced appearance mentioned by the Standard is the most difficult to define but is instantly recognizable. Balance is also remarkably easy to recognize by its absence. A balanced Golden Retriever possesses everything in proportion and is a joy to behold. So many have lovely heads and necks but then the well-developed body is set on short legs, so ruining the symmetry of the overall picture.

Many people have an eye for a dog and will instinctively know if a dog is balanced or not. Others will have to work harder to develop their perception; they know all is not right, but do not know why it is not right. I remember looking at a top-winning bitch many times from the ringside. Not only was she beautiful but she positively sparkled, yet I always felt she did not 'fill my eye'. There was something not quite right, but what it was I did not know. Later, when I had the opportunity of judging her, I found she was a little too long in the back. Although the extra length was fractional, it was enough to destroy the required balance, when viewing the whole dog.

Do not expect your teenage Golden Retriever to be balanced, as he will pass through the stage where he looks tucked-up and leggy. If he was balanced as a well-rounded puppy, then this teenage stage will be temporary and he will revert to his former symmetry.

Bitches sometimes need a litter before they appear balanced. If too much daylight is visible under the body when viewed in profile, a litter will nearly always put this right. Some very lean bitches might need two litters before they look fully mature. With male dogs, there is no way of hurrying the process; only maturity will provide the solution.

The level movement of a Golden Retriever is a joy to see. He appears to flow effortlessly round the ring. Movement does not just happen, and sound, free movement can never result from faulty construction. I remember reading a critique from an eminent judge, who said: 'This dog is built so correctly that he has to move perfectly'. Short, perpendicular upper arms will never result in long, free strides.

The desirable characteristics of a Golden Retriever are less easy to measure than the construction. You do not have to live with one of the breed very long before you realize which characteristics he possesses. At his best he is extremely biddable and will go to endless pains to please his owner. The intelligence of the breed is undeniable, to the point of being uncanny at times. His natural working ability manifests itself in the way he will carry anything from shoes and socks to cushions and large branches.

Temperament

The nature of the breed is what first attracts most people. The 'kindly' part shows when he may be trusted with small babies, toddlers and other young creatures. It has always given me enormous pleasure to see my dogs mixing with young piglets, calves and day-old chicks, none showing the slightest surprise at the others' presence. The picture of Gaineda Cinnamon Silk with a small fluffy chick perched on her head is indelibly printed on my mind. The picture of Rossbourne Angelene giving me a live mouse (which I confidently removed from her mouth, mistaking the tail for a dead leaf!) is equally vivid.

The friendly and confident characteristics show in the Golden Retriever who rushes to the door, barking loudly, covering you in licks and wagging incessantly. Some Golden Retrievers are confident to the point of being foolhardy. I have often watched my very clever Border Collie retire in despair from a group of bullock ruffians, only to see a couple of Golden Retrievers standing their ground. Farmers will admit that it is indeed a confident dog who will move young bullocks out at grass, but my lovely, gentle Orchid will do just that. Yet I have seen the same gentle bitch sit with closed eyes and a pained expression while the rasp-like tongue of a young cow licked back and forth across her muzzle.

Head and Skull

The Standard dictates that the head should be 'balanced and well-chiselled'. It is this that gives the Golden Retriever's head its very beautiful planes. A lack of chiselling makes the head appear cloddy, unattractive, and too heavy. I believe that a lack of chiselling occurs more often in the male, while some bitches have rather too much chiselling, which tends to give the appearance of a weak head and hard expression.

The six Golden Retrievers shown in the following photographs are all titles-holders and illustrate the wide variation in head and expression.

Sh.Ch. Lindys Butterscotch of Melfricka. (Photo Pearce)

Ch. Camrose Fabius Tarquin. (Photo Dog World)

24

Ch. and Ir. Ch. Cabus Cadet
(Photo Fall)

Sh.Ch. Janville Tempestuous
at Linchael.

Sh.Ch. Linchael Delmoss.

Ch. and Ir. Ch. Mandingo
Buidhe Colum.

The desired broadness of the skull should not be confused with a coarse, heavy head which is most uncharacteristic of the breed. The skull is slightly rounded but never domed. A flat skull gives a completely foreign appearance.

The 'powerful, wide and deep' muzzle is essential if the dog is to do the job he was bred for. A cock pheasant is a sizeable retrieve for any dog, but one possessing any deviation from the required muzzle would find it an impossible task. The reference to width and depth must be proportionate to the rest of the head as it should be remembered that we are striving for balance in all things.

Ideally the length of foreface should measure the same as the distance from stop to occiput. This is essentially a visual measure and I am always incredibly suspicious of judges who display great measuring techniques using finger and thumb. If these lengths are correct, your eye will tell you as well as any tape-measure.

It is quite common to find frown marks on a Golden Retriever's head and this is almost exclusive to the male. It gives a 'hang dog' look, which is quite foreign to this breed and most undesirable.

Ridges of fur known as 'calf-licks' are not infrequently found and run from the stop along the muzzle. This detracts from the gentle expression and, incidentally, crops up for generations if you breed from such animals. It may be classed as a minor fault but my personal view is that anything which detracts from the desired expression to such a degree should be classified more seriously.

The nose should be black, although some become paler in winter. A very dark nose will often be found on dogs who have very dark skin. Bitches whose noses are very pale will undergo a transforma-

Ch. Beauchasse Gaiety and Fordvale Monarch from the 1950s illustrating excellent pigmentation.

tion to the blackest pigment when they are feeding a litter. Good, dark pigment is relatively easy to breed; if the parents have it, the progeny are almost certain to inherit it.

Eyes

Eye shape and colour are of vital importance as they are prime ingredients of expression. The desired dark brown eye should be dark enough in the range of its colour, but always distinguishable from black. A black eye is expressionless and characterless but, having said that, it is preferred to the light eye, which has a vulpine appearance. A light-eyed Golden Retriever can never have that melting expression which sets it apart from other breeds. The hazel or yellow eye has a hard, calculating appearance.

The shape of the eye is important. A small eye destroys the balance of the head and a large eye is totally uncharacteristic. Any oriental eye shape is to be avoided. If the eyes are set too close together, a hard expression is the result. They should be far apart enough for their placement to appear balanced.

Dark rims are desirable and more attractive against any colour of coat. The word dark is relative, and one may move far from the dark of the nose and still have the desired eye-rim colour. It is interesting to see the colour variation in the eye rims of certain lines. My puppies have very pale, almost flesh-coloured, eye rims early on but have the darkest rims by six months. Eye-rim colour seems to have little relationship with nose colour, as dogs with jet-black noses may have pale eye rims. Some pale-nosed dogs have eye rims that look as if they have been heavily treated with Kohl pencil.

Ears

The 'moderate size' demanded by the Standard should be in proportion to the rest of the head. There is a tremendous variation in the size and shape of Golden Retrievers' ears. Some have neat, triangular flaps and some would make good hang-gliders! The texture of the ears is not mentioned in the Standard but varies enormously, even among litter-mates. Some may have thick, velvety ears. Others have fine-skinned, silky ears. My puppies have such densely pigmented ears that I frequently stop and stare in horror as the initial appearance is of black stripes on the ear edges.

Ear carriage is important. Ears should be set on so that the inner edge is more or less level with the eye. High-set ears are an abomination but low-set ears are equally ugly. Some Golden Retrievers have ears that are set on correctly but then they develop a habit of flying them when moving. This is not a fault but an undesirable habit. I have a dog who does this and I know no way of correcting it, although distracting his attention helps. Many Golden Retrievers talk with their ears. Wild Silk always greets me with a hideous grin, ears sticking straight out at the sides like handlebars. Normally her ear carriage is quite correct.

Mouth

The Golden Retriever's jaw should be strong. He is a bird-carrying dog and needs the power to fulfil his task. A weak jaw is undesirable and extremely ugly, especially when viewed in profile.

The bite (the way in which the teeth close together) should be a scissor bite. This means the top teeth fit neatly over the bottom set. The bottom teeth should touch the top teeth at the back and should be partially visible when viewed from the front.

If a dog has perfect dentition, he will have forty-two teeth. If any are missing, they will most probably be premolars, which are found immediately behind the long fang-like canine teeth. The absence of premolars is a fault in certain lines and, as it is self-perpetuating, such dogs should not be bred from. I have seldom found British

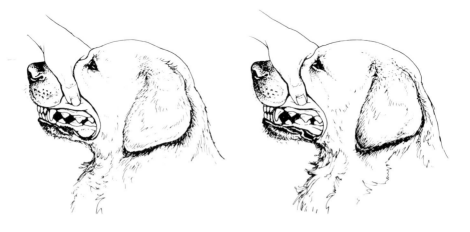

Scissor bite.   Even bite.

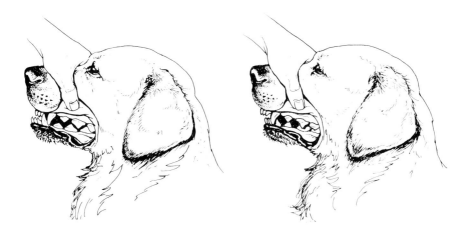

Undershot bite.   *Overshot bite.*

judges to pay much attention to the absence of teeth, but abroad it is considered a more serious fault and I have even been asked to count teeth! A dog with a missing tooth would be banned from holding a major award in some countries. In Britain, judges consider dentition as part of the whole dog, no more or less important than any other part.

Neck

The length of neck is of great visual importance when assessing a Golden Retriever's balance. If the neck is not of the correct length, it will not matter how well made the rest of the dog is – the overall picture will not be one of balance. A short necked Golden Retriever is untypical but the fault crops up quite frequently. A neck that appears short on a young Golden Retriever will look even shorter as the dog ages and thickens over the shoulders.

The neck is important in a working dog. However good at his job, the short-necked Golden Retriever will have a difficult task when he attempts to hold a hare clear of a five-barred gate. Indeed, it would be difficult for a weak-necked dog to carry anything but the smallest hen bird. There is a quality about a reachy, muscular neck which makes a Golden Retriever look every inch the thoroughbred. This quality is absent from the short-necked dog.

Ch. Dewmist Maxamillion showing excellent reach of neck.

Rachenco Charnez of Gaineda at 11 months, showing all the promise she later fulfilled. (Photo Fryckstrand)

Cleanness of neck refers to an absence of loose skin around the throat. If your Golden Retriever appears throaty, there is nothing you can do about it. Trimming very closely may reduce the fault slightly.

Forequarters

To me, the correct construction of this area is of great importance. I am fully aware that it is but one part of the dog, but it does comprise several vitally important components. It is one part of a Golden Retriever which, when faulty, is very difficult to breed out, as it seems to be self-perpetuating.

The Standard requires the legs to be straight. This means that there should be no tendency to bow or splay. Nor should the elbows be loose. There are many variations of these faults. The legs may be bowed with the feet turned out; the pasterns may be weak. It is impossible to overlook a faulty front. So many dogs, who are otherwise sound, fail in this respect.

The 'good bone' required by the Standard should be of a thickness which is in proportion to the rest of the animal. Golden Retrievers

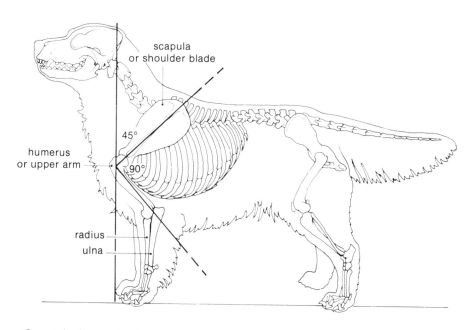

Correct shoulder construction.

with massive bone are reminiscent of Pyreneans and untypical of the breed. Some lines are naturally lighter in bone than others. Generally, there are more Goldens suffering from lack of bone than from an excess of it.

Poor shoulders are arguably the most prevalent fault in the breed. They are very easy to breed and very difficult to eradicate. If the parents have poor, or even mediocre, shoulders, the progeny will almost certainly inherit them. The Standard demands that the shoulders should be well laid back. It is a pity our Standard does not dictate the angle between the scapula (shoulder blade) and humerus (upper arm). The American Standard states an angle of 90 degrees, and this is what we are aiming for. Only then can the legs be placed in the desired way, well under the body. If the angulation is not correct, the legs will be set on like table legs – at the corners. This gives an unbalanced appearance. Only a correct degree of angulation will give the desired movement. The wider the angle becomes, the worse the resulting movement.

The length of blade and upper arm should be roughly equal. If you

Ch. Sansue Camrose Phoenix illustrating good legs, set well under the body. (Photo Pearce)

USA Ch. Charterhall Ivanhoe (the first New Zealand bred Golden Retriever to become an American Champion) possessing good construction of shoulder and upper arm.

have this in your stock, guard it carefully, as it is indeed a rare quality. Judges feel for this length of blade and the angulation where the two bones meet. I am aware of the pleasure on my face when I make the discovery of a correct assembly.

When the shoulder blades are set too wide apart, the dog will have a bossy action, which is far removed from the free, long-striding action demanded by the Standard. The shoulders should appear and feel clean, that is, without any excess muscle.

Shoulder blades that are too narrow result in the forelegs being placed too closely together so that the dog appears slab-sided when viewed from the front. This detracts from the desired balance and powerful overall appearance.

There are many top winners who possess faulty shoulders. It is possible to recognize the progeny of these animals because the fault is dominant, which means that it is more likely to be passed down than most other characteristics. It saddens me to see such dogs being used at stud and such bitches bred from. There are good dogs and bitches

Sh.Ch. Melfricka Echo showing the desired shoulder and upper arm. (Photo Dalton)

with correct shoulder construction and it makes sound sense to favour these in a breeding programme, especially in a breed in which the fault is so serious. These are strong words but there is little uglier in the Golden Retriever than poor shoulders and responsible breeders should make a real attempt to identify the fault and eradicate it.

When the dog is viewed in profile, the front legs should be straight with no tendency towards sloping pasterns. Young stock which still needs to tighten in this area may slope a little but by the time the dog is a year old, this should have rectified itself. If it is not right then, time will not correct it.

When the dog is standing or coming towards you, the elbows should be well tucked in. If they are loose, the movement will be seriously affected. Puppies and young dogs sometimes show a looseness which will correct itself with maturity. Controlled exercise will help a dog to tighten but no amount of exercise can ever rectify truly faulty construction.

Body

The general balance of the Golden Retriever has been dealt with at the beginning of this chapter. It is desirable that all parts appear in correct proportion to one another. The dog should be of a suitable height to balance his length. He should be broad enough for his height and length and deep enough to balance all the other parts. It should be remembered that we are describing the perfect dog, the one that exists in our minds. Those existing in reality will deviate slightly in some or all areas. It is the degree of deviation which is important.

The body is essentially that of a powerful, working dog. It should be well muscled, suggesting activity. Any suggestion of a cobby appearance is most undesirable, as is excessive length. Long backs are generally weak backs, and usually dip behind the shoulders. Any suggestion of this is a departure from the desired level back. Some Goldens slope which make them appear to 'drop off' over the croup. Others have a longer slope, which starts from the withers (the point where the neck and the body join). A low tail set should not be confused with a sloping back.

Ch. Catcombe Crystal, a delightful example of a well-constructed Golden Retriever.

Ch. Davern Figaro showing the correct short-coupled deep body.
(Photo Cooke)

A short-coupled body is short between the end of the ribs and the beginning of the pelvis. This is the loin. A dog who is long in the loin will appear very badly balanced. There is a definite distinction between a short-coupled dog and one who is short-backed. The former is a desirable characteristic, whereas the latter is positively undesirable. The Golden Retriever's rib-cage is not a short one but neither is it excessively long. One of the attractions of the Golden Retriever is that it is a breed free from excesses. It is possible to find specimens of the breed that are long in the rib-cage, but I have only ever found one that was short.

The shape of the ribs is important. If they are too flat (slab-sided) they are as incorrect as if they were too rounded (barrelled). The correct rib shape may be assessed by looking down on the dog and, to a lesser degree, by viewing from the front and the rear. The depth of the body bears no relation to how well sprung (rounded) the ribs are. A judge will feel for this as well as look for it. Flesh will not compensate for lack of spring of rib; only the skeleton will give the shape.

When I first judged abroad, the fact that my critiques contained the term 'slab-sided' was thought to be most odd. I tried to find an alternative description, but although I am not often lost for words, I came to the conclusion that this term simply could not be improved upon. It is totally descriptive of the dog's shape.

The ribs should be discernible by touch but not by sight. The covering of flesh should be adequate but never excessive. Any fat in this area will cause a rolling action when the dog moves.

The desired level topline of the breed is most attractive. Ideally, it will appear absolutely level when viewed in profile. The topline will have an almost imperceptible rise over the pelvis, discernible when the dog is handled. Observe the skeleton and you will realize that there must be a very slight rise at this point. The bony construction is not perfectly level so, consequently, the topline cannot feel anything but fractionally raised. An examination of the canine skeleton will prove this point, and excellent examples may be found in veterinary textbooks.

The Standard requires the Golden Retriever to be deep through the heart. This depth is obvious in profile and from the front. It is possible for dogs to be too deep or too shallow. The dog who is too deep appears short in the leg and cloddy. This is a deviation from the

Sh.Ch. Lindys Butterscotch of Melfricka, a dog of excellent depth. (Photo Pearce)

active and powerful appearance which is the ideal. The over-deep body makes the legs appear too short and so the overall balance is ruined.

A body that is too shallow also detracts from the required powerful appearance. It should never resemble the construction of the Chesapeake Bay Retriever. A shallow body makes the legs look overlong. This combination could never result in an impression of power.

The tail set can add to, or detract from, the impression of a level topline but the two features are quite distinct. The topline can be perfectly correct when the tail set is faulty. The ideal position is for the tail set to be level with the back. When the dog is moving, the tail should never be carried above this level. Do not be confused by pictures of posed Golden Retrievers which show the tail sticking straight in line with the back, like a poker. Even if you cannot see the hand holding the tip, you can be sure it was there and has been masked by the photographer. The way in which the tail appears to be set on in a photograph may be very different from the way it is in reality.

Ch. Sansue Golden Ruler showing a perfectly straight topline and excellent tail carriage. (Photo Bull)

A high-set tail may be disguised by a skilful handler when the dog is standing still, but it is virtually impossible to disguise on the move. Handlers employ all sorts of methods to disguise the carriage but they can never alter the set. A dog who carries his tail above the level of the back is said to be 'gay tailed'. It is an ugly fault as it destroys the balance of the outline but, like all other faults, it should be viewed as part of the whole dog.

A low-set tail is impossible to disguise either when the dog is standing or moving. In both cases, he will appear to 'rake off' (slope) over the croup. Again, it is an ugly fault but should not be viewed in isolation. There have been title-holders made up with both low and high tail sets.

The tail should never curl at the tip. The tail naturally grows a profuse covering of hair. In Britain it is traditional to trim the fringe or 'feathering' on the tail. The tip should be rounded to reach the hock or just below. The hair should then be trimmed so that it is at its longest at the base of the tail (around 5 inches) and becomes progressively shorter towards the tip. Chapter 5 on trimming deals more fully with this (*see* pages 86–95).

Hindquarters

The hindquarters propel the dog and should suggest both power and strength. The impression of strength begins with the comparatively short and muscular construction of the loin.

As the dog moves away, the hocks provide the drive. The overall picture should be four-square with no tendency for the hocks to turn in or out. If his hocks are constructed correctly, he will move accordingly. When viewed from behind, the hocks should appear parallel. The term 'hock' covers the area extending from the top of the foot to the first joint.

Dogs may have faulty hocks for several reasons. Good rearing plays an important part in the formation of sound hocks. If the puppy has been brought up in a pen which had a solid part at the bottom of the run, topped by bars or wire, it is a reasonable assumption that he will have spent a large proportion of his time standing up, looking out. This will put undue stress on the hocks and may result in weak hocks which turn inwards. Such an animal is said to be 'cow-hocked'. I can only assume that the cows of yesteryear were constructed differently from their modern counterparts, since my cows have hocks that would be desirable for a Golden Retriever!

*A natural study of Ch. Nortonwood Faunus illustrating powerful
quarters. (Photo Bradbury)*

There are many terms which may be applied to hocks, perhaps
more than to any other part of the body. If a dog's hocks are so
acutely angled that the foot is set too far under the body, he is said to
be over-angulated in the hock. In a long-hocked dog, the distance
between the top of the foot (where a heel would be) and the hock-
joint is disproportionately long. A sickle-hocked dog has hocks that
curve, so causing the back part of the foot to be walked on and not
the front pads. This is another sign of weakness. Thinly boned
hocks, which totally detract from a picture of power are called
spindle hocks. If there is little or no angulation where the hock meets
the joint, the dog may be described as 'straight in the hock'. This is a
fault in construction and rearing has no influence on this condition.

An over-angulated hock results from too great a slope from the
hock-joint to the ground. As in the sickle hock, the foot is set too far
under the body but the hock itself is not bowed. A short-hocked dog
has too little space between the foot and the joint. This will make him
appear too low on the leg and will certainly affect the desired free-
striding action.

There is little doubt that other factors resulting in incorrect hocks

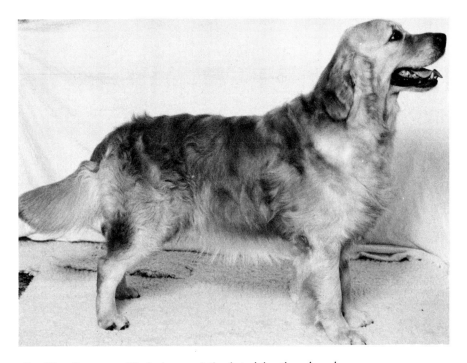

Ch. Okus Buccaneer. His hocks are of the desired length and angle.
(Photo Platt)

include faulty nutrition, incorrect exercise but, most of all, heredity. Dogs possessing faulty hocks mated with bitches possessing similar faults will produce these problems in their offspring. This cause may be avoided by researching the hock status of not only sire and dam, but also the grandparents.

The Standard demands 'well-bent stifles'. The stifle is the point where the femur meets the fibula/tibia. This is directly related to the front angulation and, almost without exception, if the dog's front angulation is correct, so will be the rear angulation. The greater the angle between the femur and tibia, the straighter the stifle. A dog will never have the desired free-striding action, enabling him to cover the ground, if he possesses straight stifles.

There are examples in the breed of straight stifles and over-angulated stifles. The latter, when viewed in profile, cause the dog to appear as if he is attempting to kneel. Such exaggerations are faults and should be avoided. Both faults are self-perpetuating, which means that they appear in the progeny of such dogs with certainty.

Hindquarters that are correctly constructed but insufficiently muscled will appear out of proportion with the rest of the dog. When dogs become old, there is a falling away of musculature, but, in their prime, Golden Retrievers should have sufficient muscle to fill out the quarters. This should never be confused with excess flesh: muscle feels hard to the touch whereas fat allows your fingers to sink into it.

The feet should be 'round and cat-like'. The Golden Retriever's foot, at its best, is most attractive. The toes are well arched and tight against one another. If the toes tend to be extended rather than close and arched, road work will help, but it will never change a poor foot into a good one. A long, flat foot, making the dog appear to tread on his heels, is called a 'hare-foot'. Good feet and poor feet are present in certain strains. Care should be taken to breed a bitch possessing mediocre or poor feet to a dog whose feet are correct and whose parents had good feet.

A sound Golden Retriever will move with much drive from the quarters. The legs and feet move in a parallel fashion with no tendency to converge. The stride is free and long and there is no hint of hackney action in front. I wish there were many such dogs but regrettably Golden Retrievers today move badly. Many show sharply converging instead of parallel lines at both ends. I maintain that if the width of a Golden Retriever's leg set in front is narrow, it will give rise to a slight converging of lines when he moves but the emphasis is on the word 'slight'. Many Golden Retrievers pin-toe or show a tendency for the feet to diverge from the perpendicular. Some also lift their feet very high when moving. If the dog is correctly built, his hindquarters should propel him forwards in a long, free stride. Any undue lifting of the forelegs will only impede this freedom.

When a dog is loose in the elbows, this will result in his throwing out his legs on the move. A correctly constructed forehand will result in his moving in a straight line with little divergence from the perpendicular.

A Golden Retriever is said to 'plait' if he walks inside the central line of balance. This happens when the dog, on coming towards you, places one foot inside the other.

Bad movement may be unilateral. It is quite possible to find a Golden Retriever with one good, straight foreleg while the other turns out instead of facing forwards when moving. A Golden Retriever who moves correctly is a joy to watch and appears to be

Correct front – standing.

Out at elbow.

'Plaiting' in front.

One front foot turning out.

Both feet turning out.

Correct front – moving.

flowing along. The gait appears quite effortless. He will take an increase of speed in his stride, preferring this to any tendency to bound along. Good movement appears to be controlled and is visually pleasing.

One frequently finds Golden Retrievers who are 'close behind'. This is the term used to describe the hind legs moving in close proximity to each other. It is more unusual, but quite possible, to observe those who move 'wide behind', which is the opposite problem.

The Golden Retriever's coat is his most glamorous attribute. Little is more attractive than a fully coated Golden Retriever gleaming in the sunshine. The hair may be flat or wavy but never curled. Some spayed bitches develop very curly coats. The hair should be neither coarse nor silky but the texture should fall between the two. The top hairs are longer and the undercoat dense and fluffy. Only dogs possessing real undercoats will be waterproof when working.

The flatter type of coat is by far the easiest to prepare for show. It is possible for a dog with a coat of this texture to appear neat and tidy immediately after shampooing followed by a light towelling. The heavy, wavy coat will need brushing and combing dry and some

The Golden Retriever's coat is his most glamorous attribute.
Nor. Ch. Linchael Conclusion, aged 15 months. (Photo Fryckstrand)

resort to pinning a towel over the dog in an attempt to persuade the hair to lie in as orderly a fashion as possible. Such coats are a nightmare to prepare for the show ring, but look spectacular when well presented.

The heavier the coat, the more likely you are to bath the dog well before the show. Such coats take several days to settle and will not appear to advantage if newly bathed. The gloss takes several days to be restored following bathing.

When a dog is said to be 'out of coat' the whole undercoat comes out and makes the dog appear considerably skinnier. Dogs vary in the way they moult. With some, the skin is visible and with others the moult is so slight that they can be shown throughout the year. If you have a dog who undergoes a complete moult, there is nothing you can do but wait for the new coat to appear, which takes about three months. Never do dogs moult as heavily as they do when you have just entered them for several Championship Shows! You can aid the process of growing a new coat by combing out the dead hair and brushing daily to stimulate the new growth. I find that oil of evening primrose capsules ensure that the new hair carries a good sheen.

Coat colour has given rise to strong words, both verbal and in print. The Standard states quite clearly: 'Any shade of gold or cream, neither red nor mahogany'. I have seen several Golden Retrievers who were too dark to fit the Standard but I have never seen one who was too pale. I have also seen critiques, written by quite experienced judges, which have stated, 'Coat of correct gold colour', which suggests that the rest of the colour range is incorrect. I have also seen and heard reference being made to the number of 'white' Golden Retrievers in the ring today. I can honestly say that I have never seen a white one. However pale a Golden Retriever is, stand him next to a Samoyed and observe the difference. For many years I have shown cream dogs on white leads to stress this difference.

Modern exhibitors will assume that I favour the paler Golden Retrievers but those who know better will realize that I have bred champions in all the accepted colours. It is also interesting to observe just how many Challenge Certificates I have awarded to Golden Retrievers at the darker end of the scale abroad. My personal preference is for as dark a coat as is permissible, preferably with lighter feathering. Those who remember Deerflite Destiny at Linchael would have seen my ideal. I stress, however, that this is a personal preference and such feelings have no place in the show ring.

45

The judge must adhere to the directive of the Standard, and the dog who conforms most closely to this must be the winner, irrespective of whether he is cream, mid- or dark golden. It is a pity that one of the breed's greatest attributes, the colour, is often the cause of much dissent.

Height and Weight

The current Standard does not dictate weight, so we must use our discretion. The Golden Retriever is essentially both powerful and active. He cannot fulfil these requirements if he is overweight. The condition of the dog is an important factor when assessing weight. Well-boned dogs will obviously be heavier than lightly boned animals. A Golden Retriever's weight will fluctuate through the year. A male will lose weight when he is used at stud on a regular basis and when bitches around him are in season. Bitches tend to gain and lose weight according to their seasons. Some mature bitches who produce just a few puppies in a litter have a tendency to retain extra weight. Bitches feeding large litters will lose weight alarmingly, however you feed them.

As an approximate guide, bitches in show condition should weigh around 65 pounds (29.5 kg) and dogs should be 10 pounds (4.5 kg) heavier. The appearance of the dog is all-important. If he looks right for his age and height, his weight will be correct irrespective of what the scales read.

Size is clearly stated in the Standard at 56–61 cm (22–24 in) for dogs and bitches 51-56 cm (20-22 in). It may be seen from these measurements that a bitch of top size will measure the same as a dog at the bottom end of the scale. Size is very deceptive: Golden Retrievers who are immature and rangy in appearance will give a false impression of being taller than their mature, compact counterparts. The way in which the body properties are distributed is all-important when assessing size. Nordic Ch. Mjaerumhogda's Crusader was frequently referred to as 'small' whereas my Gaineda Counterfeiter of Somley was almost without exception called 'tall'. The two dogs were of identical height. Crusader was extremely compact but Counterfeiter was considerably longer. One should not be too hasty in deciding whether or not a dog is too short or too tall. I have come across several well-known show Golden Retrievers who were too tall. I have never seen one who was too short.

A well-known exhibitor in the mid 1960s was so tired of having her dog called 'small' that she painted inches on her stockings. When the dog stood against her, his height was instantly obvious. Eccentric maybe, but it proved her point and amused many of us, although one determined exhibitor was heard to remark, 'Everyone knows nylon stretches!'

We do not actually use a measuring stick in the ring (as happens with Poodles), so the assessment of height is a purely visual skill. It is a good mental exercise to rank your own dogs in height-order and then measure them; the results are quite surprising. If you are to judge, you need to have in your mind an indelible picture of what dogs and bitches of the correct height look like.

Faults

When the construction of a dog differs from the requirements of the Standard, that dog possesses a fault. It is important to bear in mind that the Standard states that 'the seriousness with which the fault should be regarded should be in exact proportion to its degree'. Having borne that in mind, you are left with the decision as to whether, for instance, a gay tail is a more serious fault, or a pale eye is less serious, than splay feet. They are all faults, neither more nor less important than one another. If the degree of the fault is so great that it affects movement, it would obviously be considered a serious fault. The judge is looking for how closely the dog fits the Standard; he is not making an assessment of how many faults each dog possesses. To fault-judge is quite wrong and suggests incompetence. It is possible for a Golden Retriever possessing faults to win many top awards. In fact, I cannot think of any Golden Retriever who does not possess a fault. If the dog with the less than perfect front is still better than any other dog in the class, then, irrespective of this fault, he will be placed ahead of all the others. However, there is no rule which says he must be first: it is perfectly permissible for a judge to withhold any prize, or even the Challenge Certificate, but it is an unusual occurrence in this breed and one would have to be able to account for one's actions before making such a move.

In some countries, the possession of a reasonably serious fault (e.g. incomplete dentition) would prevent that dog from winning a major award. In Britain, I have observed champions with such faults, so conclude that we are more lenient here.

I am frequently asked by new owners if their Golden Retrievers may be exhibited as they possess one fault. My somewhat facetious reply is, 'Only one?'. Many seem to think an off-black nose is a factor that will prevent them from showing their dogs. I can only reiterate that the Standard describes the ideal, and such a dog has yet to be born.

Originally, the British Breed Standard was adopted by America but they now have a much more comprehensive Standard of their own.

The American Breed Standard

(Reproduced by kind permission of the American Kennel Club)

General Appearance

A symmetrical, powerful active dog, sound and well put together, not clumsy nor long in the leg, displaying a kindly expression and possessing a personality that is eager, alert and self-confident. Primarily a hunting dog, he should be shown in hard working

Am. and Can. Ch. Jagersbo Meadowpond Melody Am. and Can. C.D. – a Golden Retriever Club of America Outstanding Dam. (Photo Booth)

condition. Overall appearance, balance, gait and purpose to be given more emphasis than any of his component parts.

Head

Broad in skull, slightly arched laterally and longitudinally without prominence of frontal bones or occipital bones. Stop well defined but not abrupt. Foreface deep and wide, nearly as long as skull. Muzzle straight in profile, blending smoothly and strongly into skull; when viewed in profile or from above, slightly deeper and wider at stop than at tip. No heaviness in flews. Removal of whiskers is permitted but not preferred.

Eyes

Friendly and intelligent in expression, medium size with dark, close-fitting rim, set well apart and reasonably deep in sockets. Color preferably dark brown, medium brown acceptable. Slant eyes and narrow, triangular eyes detract from correct expression and are to be faulted. No white or haw visible when looking straight ahead. Dogs showing function abnormality of eyelids or eyelashes (such as, but not limited to, trichiasis, entropion, ectropion or distichiasis) are to be excused from the ring.

Nose

Black or brownish in color, though fading to a lighter shade in cold weather not serious. Pink nose or one seriously lacking in pigmentation to be faulted.

Ears

Rather short with front edge attached well behind and just above the eye and falling close to cheek. When pulled forward, tip of ear should just cover the eye. Low, hound-like ear set to be faulted.

Neck

Medium long, merging gradually into well-laid-back shoulders, giving sturdy muscular appearance. Untrimmed natural ruff. No throatiness.

Body

Well balanced, short coupled, deep through chest. Chest between forelegs at least as wide as a man's closed hand, including thumb, with well-developed forechest.

Brisket extends to elbows. Ribs long and well sprung but not barrel-shaped, extending well towards hindquarters. Loin short, muscular, wide and deep with very little tuck-up. Back line strong and level from withers to slightly sloping croup whether standing or moving. Slab-sidedness, narrow chest, lack of depth in brisket, sloping back line, roach or sway back, excessive tuck-up, flat or steep croup to be faulted.

Forequarters

Muscular, well co-ordinated with hindquarters, and capable of free movement. Shoulder blades long and well laid back with upper tips fairly close together at withers. Upper arms appear about the same length as the blades, setting the elbows back beneath the upper tip of the blades, close to the ribs without looseness. Legs viewed from the front, straight with good bone but not to the point of coarseness. Pasterns short and strong, sloping slightly with no suggestion of weakness.

Hindquarters

Broad and strong muscled. Profile of croup slopes slightly; the pelvic bone slopes at a slightly greater angle (approximately 30 degrees from the horizontal). In a natural stance, the femur joins the pelvis at approximately a 90 degrees angle; stifles well bent; hocks well let down with short, strong neat pasterns. Legs straight when viewed from rear. Cow hocks, spread hocks and sickle hocks to be faulted.

Feet

Medium size, round and compact and well knuckled, with thick pads. Excess hair may be trimmed to show size and contour. Dewclaws on forelegs may be removed but are normally left on. Splay or hare feet to be faulted.

Am. and Can. Ch. Thornfield Lark O' Meadowpond – a Golden Retriever Club of America Outstanding Dam. (Photo Broadbeck)

Tail

Well set on, thick and muscular at the base, following the natural line of the croup. Tail bones extend to, but not below, the point of the hock carried with a merry action, level with or some moderate upward curve, never curled over back or between legs.

Coat

Dense and water repellant with good undercoat. Outer coat firm and resilient, neither coarse nor silky, lying close to body; may be straight or wavy. Moderate feathering on back of forelegs and on under-body; heavier feathering on front of neck, back of thighs and underside of tail. Coat on head, paws and front of legs is short and even. Excessive length, open coats and limp, soft coats are very undesirable. Feet may be trimmed and stray hair neatened, but the natural appearance of coat or outline should not be altered by cutting or clipping.

Am. and Can. Ch. Sugarbear's Echo of Hillkirk CD, WC. (Photo Kernan)

Color

Rich, lustrous golden of various shades. Feathering may be lighter than rest of coat. With the exception of greying or whitening of face or body due to age, any white marking, other than a few white hairs on the chest, should be penalized according to its extent. Allowable light shadings not to be confused with white marking. Predominant body color which is extremely pale or extremely dark is undesirable. Some latitude should be given to the light puppy whose coloring shows promise of deepening with maturity. Any noticeable area of black or other off-color hair is a serious fault.

Gait

When trotting, gait is free, smooth, powerful and well co-ordinated, showing good reach. Viewed from any position, legs turn neither in nor out, nor do feet cross or interfere with each other. As speed increases, feet tend to converge towards centre line of balance. It is recommended that dogs be shown on a loose lead to reflect true gait.

Size

Males 23–24 inches in height at withers; females $21\frac{1}{2}$–$22\frac{1}{2}$ inches. Dogs of up to one inch above or below standard size should be proportionately penalized. Deviation in height of more than one inch from the Standard shall disqualify. Length from breastbone to point of buttocks slightly greater than height at withers in ratio of 12:11. Weight of dogs 65–75 lbs; bitches 55–65 lbs.

Temperament

Friendly, reliable and trustworthy. Quarrelsomeness or hostility towards other dogs or people in normal situations, or an unwarranted show of timidity or nervousness, is not in keeping with Golden Retriever character. Such actions should be penalized according to their significance.

Faults

Any departure from the described ideal shall be considered faulty to the degree to which it interferes with the breed's purpose or is contrary to breed character.

Disqualifications

1. Deviation in height of more than one inch from Standard either way.
2. Undershot or overshot bite.

3
Buying your Puppy

When you first consider buying a puppy, it is a very sound idea to examine the reasons why you should not have one. I always point out all these reasons to prospective buyers, as it is far better for them to decide at this stage that perhaps a dog is not for them than decide when they have reached home with their new charge.

However much you like dogs, there are certain drawbacks to owning one. They need constant attention and companionship. Even if you keep your puppy meticulously clean, he will bring his own particular brand of mud and fluff into your home. If you live in a house furnished with priceless antiques and sumptuous Chinese rugs, then think again! Your puppy is unable to differentiate between cheap rugs and those costing enormous sums. Neither can he tell the difference between the legs of a Chippendale chair and those of a kitchen stool. Both are equally good to chew. If you do have a beautifully furnished home and go demented at the sight of a tuft of dog hair clinging to the sofa, do not go ahead with your acquisition of a puppy thinking that he can be kennelled outside. Kennelling for short periods will not harm your Golden Retriever but kennelling on a permanent basis will make him frustrated and unhappy. Unless he can be your companion for most of his life, then, out of kindness to him, put his interests before your indulgence.

Dogs need regular exercise and while this might conjure up visions of idyllic walks along sunny country lanes, consider carefully the less pleasant spectacle of tramping through mud in driving rain on a cold winter's morning, and then again on an equally unpleasant night. Dogs need walks irrespective of the day, weather, state of your health or appearance of visitors. I can illustrate this by recalling a remark made by a visitor one Christmas. She said, 'Do you really feed the cows today?' This remark struck me as amusing at the time but on reflection I realized just how little some people understand the needs of animals. It is our duty to bend our activities to accommodate their routine, never the other way around.

*If you are a keen gardener you will need to examine the pros
and cons of acquiring a puppy!*

A puppy in the house means someone must always be available at his mealtimes. If you have a busy social life, this could interfere with your arrangements. A hungry puppy cannot understand, and should not be expected to tolerate, your irregular appearances which cause him to deviate from his accepted mealtimes.

Holiday arrangements are never the same again once you have a dog as a member of the family. Holidays formerly spent lazing abroad in the sun are now spent walking in the countryside, or staying in hotels where dogs are accepted. Even this may be drastically interrupted if your bitch decides to come into season the night before your holiday. You then face the prospect of cancelling your holiday or booking her into boarding kennels. In the height of the summer season, it is quite difficult to find kennels with a last-minute vacancy and kennelling will also add extra to the cost of your holiday.

If you are a keen gardener, you will need to examine the pros and cons of acquiring a puppy extra carefully. Speaking from experience, it *is* possible to keep a dog and a garden in perfect harmony, but it takes a lot of organization and planning. My own dogs come and go through the drive gates and the kitchen door, from where they have access to a farmyard and a five-acre paddock. My garden and greenhouses occupy a large site to the front and side of the house, so the dogs need never pass through. In the early days, I had a misguided belief that one could have a lovely garden to be enjoyed by both humans and dogs. It didn't work! They dug holes in the lawn, pulled the labels off plants, chewed 'sticks', which were expensive shrubs, beheaded flowers and, to the consternation of my Koi Carp, swam in the pond. Not a happy memory!

There is also the not unimportant consideration of your car. Owning a dog will completely revolutionize your ideas about cars. As a former lover and owner of two-seater sports cars, which were traded in for 'suitable' estate cars, I write with a certain measure of nostalgia. No longer will your first consideration be your car's looks or performance; now you will calculate how many dogs could comfortably lie in the back and which colour upholstery will render paw marks and hair invisible.

Lastly, you must remember that owning a dog can be expensive. Quite aside from the initial outlay, there is the cost of feeding him for the twelve or more years of his life. In addition, provision must be made for vet's bills. However healthy your dog is, there will be occasions throughout his life when visits to the vet are necessary. To help with the unexpected vet's bill it is worth considering some of

Why choose a Golden Retriever? Some of Rayne Rowe's Golden Retrievers showing the appeal of the breed. From top left to right: Sh.Ch. Raynesgold Rifleman, Raynesgold Repose and Raynesgold Vanrose Versatile. Centre: Raynesgold Rightaway. Bottom: Raynesgold Rainorshine, Raynesgold Glennessa Etoile and Mitzi. (Photo Cheltenham Newspaper Co. Ltd)

the pet insurance schemes that are available. (*See also* page 66.)

If you still want a dog, why should you choose a Golden Retriever? There are many good, all-round, family dogs but for me none is as attractive as the Golden Retriever.

I once heard the breed described as 'a dog for all reasons' and was impressed by this description. He is a willing worker, both with the gun and in obedience competition. As a house dog he is superb, as he will give vocal warning of the approach of strangers but is hardly ever aggressive. He will willingly and enthusiastically join in teenage games but is equally happy visiting elderly relatives, where he sits quietly to be patted.

For me the choice of a Golden Retriever was made because I wanted to own a breed that was both beautiful and intelligent. My resolve was strengthened when I came across Mrs K. Needs' Obedience Champion Castelnau Pizzicato. I thought he was the loveliest dog I had ever seen. He was always alert and ready to obey commands but was also the most delightfully affectionate companion. Little did Mrs Needs know that my acquaintance with her dog was to start this obsession that many years later shows no signs of abating!

Finding a Breeder

Once you have decided on a Golden Retriever as the breed for you, do *not* go to a kennel that sells various breeds. Some of these are bought in from elsewhere instead of being bred on the premises and the risk of infection is greater.

The secretaries of breed clubs, listed at the end of this book (*see* Appendices 1 and 2), will provide you with a list of reputable breeders in your area. My own definition of a reputable breeder is one who breeds from stock that is eye tested and hip scored, of sound temperament and that conforms as closely to the Breed Standard as possible. Further proof of a breeder's repute can be seen in well-reared, well-fed puppies kept in clean, pleasant conditions.

Having obtained a list of breeders in your area, ring or write, stating what you want. I prefer people to write in the first instance. If they ring when I am trimming or bathing a dog, I cannot give them my full attention. It is very important to say whether you want a dog for a pet, for show or for work. If you just want one because you like the breed but have no aspirations towards the show ring, then do not be ashamed to say so. Many top breeders begin like that. State whether you want a dog or bitch and, above all, be prepared to wait for your puppy. It is possible to get any Golden Retriever tomorrow, but the one of your choice will take a little longer.

If you know you want to show your Golden Retriever, attend shows and sit at the ringside with a catalogue. This lists the dogs and their owners and also shows the names of each dog's sire and dam. You can record the class placings in this booklet. Do not base your decision on the results of one show as you should bear in mind that results are merely a reflection of one person's opinion on one day. The next weekend, all may, and often does, change. Go to several shows and note not only which dogs win but which type you like. Also note which breeder regularly produces winners for others. The yardstick by which I measure the success of a kennel is whether it can breed winners for other owners on a regular basis. Most established breeders can win with their own stock, but do other exhibitors win with it?

Having decided that a puppy from a particular kennel is for you, contact the breeder. Please show a sound sense of timing, otherwise you may be rebuffed. I will never forget a delightful lady from abroad approaching me just as I was about to challenge for Best of Breed at Cruft's. She caught my arm and said, 'What are your immediate plans?' My reply was, 'To win Best of Breed'. When I had done so, I settled to a long conversation about my breeding plans with this lady. She said she did not mind waiting for a puppy, which proved a wise decision as the puppy she eventually had from me quickly became a champion.

Most breeders will invite you home to see their adult stock and you can discuss your needs with them in more detail then. Having made an appointment to visit the kennel of your choice, do try to keep to the time as closely as possible. If this sounds fussy, take into account that kennels are busy places and if they function efficiently, have timetables which need to be closely adhered to. My fifteen adult Golden Retrievers cannot understand that dinner is late today because they are being admired by prospective puppy owners. It is up to you to avoid feeding times rather than placing the onus on the breeder to bend his routine around you. Try to plan your arrival between mealtimes and after exercise. This way you will see the dogs at their best when they are contented and relaxed.

Try to be reasonable about how many people you take with you to visit. Most visitors bring a companion but it is stretching the hospitality of the kennel proprietor to bring all the children and grandparents.

Choosing your Puppy

Be quite open with the breeder about your requirements. If you want a pet, do not be reluctant to say so, fearing you might be given an inferior puppy. Sometimes, admitting you want a pet might be mutually beneficial. I receive hardly any enquiries for pets, although in most litters I produce at least one puppy that I consider to be of pet quality. In my most recent litter I had one who was just smaller than the rest, as frequently occurs in a large litter. She was not of show quality but was very healthy and had the most delightfully affectionate, outgoing personality. She went to a family who had just lost a Golden Retriever with heart failure. I was delighted because they were just the sort of people I wanted to own her and their delight was twofold: first, she cost far less than they would have paid for a show-quality puppy and, second, they had a puppy that was well-bred and healthy. If you want a show puppy, be specific. Tell the breeder what your ambition is and listen to his advice. No reputable breeder will knowingly mislead you. My rule is that I never allow a puppy to go for show if I would not be perfectly happy to show it myself. After all, the breeder's shop-window is the showring, so it would be foolish to let a bad advertisement for your kennel appear there.

Choosing a puppy for show is very little different from choosing one as a pet. Only the finer details will set it apart. Ideally, the puppy you choose, whether for show or as a pet, will be bold and affectionate. He should appear nicely rounded without being too fat. His eyes and ears should be clean, with no discharge or odour. His coat at the eight-weeks stage will be fluffy, bearing little resemblance to an adult coat. The skin should feel loose and there should be no evidence of parasitic infection (which manifests itself as small scabs which are easily felt by running your fingers through the coat against the way the hair lies). Watch the puppy running around. His forelegs should be straight. Do not confuse the presence of obvious 'knuckles' as deviating from straightness. A definite knuckle needs to be present at this stage as this will grow out and provide the length of the leg later. He should stand four-square with a level back, very slightly arched over the croup (the Breed Standard demands a level topline, but the skeleton dictates that there should be a very slight rise over the hip girdle).

I am suspicious of puppies who carry their tails either very low or too high when they are running about, although it is perfectly normal for them to raise their tails when feeding. I believe this is a territorial stance. They also raise their tails when indulging in mock fights with their litter-mates or dam. Tails set too high or too low in a show dog are an abomination. It is a feature that I cannot overlook. I have a top-winning Golden Retriever whose tail is carried high at home (never in the show ring). I can never look beyond this. To me the balance of the Golden Retriever is all and a gaily carried tail just destroys it.

Balance is hard to define but like many qualities, it is quite obvious when it is lacking. Balance is proportion. If your puppy is correctly proportioned, he will appear balanced. The length of his body in relation to his height is important. It is also important that you realize that during the puppy period of rapid growth, these proportions are ever changing. My puppies are at their most balanced at three and five weeks of age. All my own winners have been chosen at this stage. From six weeks onwards they become increasingly badly balanced until the adult proportions are reached and they regain their balance. You need to have the courage of your convictions, that what you saw at five weeks was what you wanted. You will not get many chances, as each day these proportions change.

Be guided by your breeder. He knows his own stock and will be able to give a reliable estimate regarding the puppy's show potential and, having a sound knowledge of his own line, should be able to show you adult stock which resembled the puppy at that age. This will give you a reasonable idea of what your puppy should grow into.

Of all the questions I am asked, the most frequent one is, 'How can I be sure the puppy I pick will be the best one?' The honest and only answer is that you cannot, but you can shorten the odds. I can only tell you the way I pick my puppies and I am quite aware that a dozen breeders writing about this would do it quite differently. It is a very personal thing, and I can only say that it has worked for me.

The first thing I do is watch them when they are newly born. There is always at least one that catches my eye. At first they all appear rather long and thin but once they have had a good feed, the illusion of length disappears and they look more balanced and rounded. As they are feeding, the necks arch and an excellent reach of neck will be apparent even when they are just a few hours old.

The type of head they have at first is virtually unrecognizable as the beautiful head the grown adult will eventually possess. I remember when my first litter was born, I could not believe how short the muzzles were. It did not occur to me then that all the wrinkling would grow out to form the eventual length of the muzzle.

During the next few weeks, I like to look at them when they are lying contentedly on their sides. At this time the shape of the puppy is clearly visible. Most breeders have a fetish and mine is for shoulder angulation. I believe that the angulation which is obvious at this stage will remain. A shoulder that is not laid back early on never will be. Neither will a short, perpendicular upper arm ever turn miraculously into one of correct length and angulation. Poor shoulders and upper arms are a serious fault in our breed. Many otherwise good champion dogs and bitches possess poor shoulders. This in itself is regrettable but it is even more so when two animals with such a fault are mated together. It is a difficult fault to breed out and when both parents possess it, it is a reasonable guarantee that the offspring will be similarly constructed. Good shoulders are a rare asset!

The head shape of puppies varies enormously with different lines. The rule I apply is to avoid any evidence of excess. By this, I mean I would be suspicious of a puppy whose head appeared exaggerated in any way. A heavy skull will result in a foreign expression, far

Head shape varies enormously with different lines.

removed from the kind, gentle one which is desirable. An obvious, but not overdone, bump on the top of the head (the prominent occiput bone) is perfectly acceptable at this stage, because when the head 'breaks' (grows), this extra height will eventually form the width of the skull.

A puppy's ears always appear too large, often giving the impression of a wash-leather at each side of the head! Do not pay too much attention to the ear size as the puppy will grow into his ears: one day you realize that they fit the rest of him and that he has lost his Dumbo appearance. Ears should be well set. That means not too high, which makes the adult expression too alert and rather hard. Neither must they be too low set, which makes the dog appear houndy.

Eye colour has many novice owners worried. Golden Retriever puppies have blue-grey eyes. This colour gradually changes to the permanent dark brown over a period of weeks. During this period, the changing colours can be very strange, but this is only temporary. I have heard tales of vaccinations temporarily affecting the eye colour but have never, personally, witnessed it in a Golden Retriever.

Eye shape is important too. At eight weeks, the eye should be in proportion to the size of the head. Eyes that are too round and prominent, or too small, give an undesirable expression. Whilst the eye rims should be black, I find my puppies have very pale rims at this stage but they always darken by the time they have their permanent teeth.

The bite (the way in which the teeth fit) in young puppies is confusing even to the expert. The desired formation is where the bottom teeth lie just behind but still touching the upper set. Even the most experienced breeders have got it wrong at some time. What seems like a good mouth at eight weeks can go drastically wrong. With my particular line, the top teeth virtually cover the lower at eight weeks old. Other breeders have told me that they would be horrified if their puppies' mouths looked like this at eight weeks, as they would almost certainly be incorrect in the adult. I can only say that all my puppies look like this at eight weeks and I am aware of breeding only two incorrect mouths in almost thirty years.

The eight-week-old puppy should have good bone. This means the legs should appear strong and rounded, more like tree trunks than saplings. The foot of the adult Golden Retriever should be cat-like but few puppies exhibit anything approaching feline feet. They are normally flatter than is desirable in an adult and soft in condition. Avoid a long or splay foot as it is unlikely to correct itself.

When viewed from the front the puppy should stand four-square. The legs should be straight without any obvious tendency to turn in or out. The elbows should be reasonably well tucked in although a degree of looseness is acceptable at this stage. Viewed from the side, the puppy should appear short-coupled. At five weeks I find the topline is what it will eventually be in adulthood. After that, the growth rate of the puppy is uneven. Sometimes the front will grow faster, making the shoulder considerably higher than the hindquarters. But if the puppy was level at five weeks, all will revert to normal eventually.

A low-set tail will never correct itself; neither will one that is too high. He is stuck with his tail carriage for life. Any deviation from the correct tail carriage alters the whole balance of the animal and I consider it a serious fault, not to be tolerated in a show puppy.

The hindquarters of my puppies revert in adulthood to what they were at five weeks. Of course, they develop muscle but the shape is laid down at this early age. A straight stifle might improve but it will never make a well-bent one, although a skilled handler is able to make a straight one appear acceptable.

My final choice is made by sitting in the pen and watching the puppies run about. If you find it almost impossible to decide between two, my advice is to take the one that appeals to you most. The reason may be its lovely expression, its free movement or just its outgoing personality. Whatever it is, be guided by what you feel, your 'gut reaction', if you can split them no other way.

Having chosen your puppy, ascertain when the puppies may leave their mother. Most leave at eight or nine weeks. Obtain a list of foodstuff and anything else you require in the way of bedding. You will also need a feeding chart. Find out when the puppy should have its first injection and if the breeder has already arranged for it to have one before it leaves. Contact your vet for an appointment in good time *before* the puppy needs its first injection.

I never cease to be amazed by the stories of what goes wrong with the documentation of litters. Most of the pitfalls can be avoided if the correct procedure is followed. The breeder should register the puppies (*see* the chapter on breeding, page 150), and I do this at about ten days when I am reasonably sure they will all survive. When you collect your puppy you should be handed its pedigree form, filled in and signed by the breeder. You should also be handed a Kennel Club Registration Certificate. This corresponds with a human birth certificate and shows the puppy's name, date of birth, sire and dam, date of registration, breeder's name and address and, most importantly, the puppy's registration number. On the back of this form is a space for the new owner's name and address, which formally transfers the puppy when the Kennel Club receives this and the appropriate fee. This transfer must have taken place before your Golden Retriever may be shown or bred from.

I always give my new puppy owners a starter pack of food. I do this for two reasons: first, it reassures me that the puppy is going to continue with the food it has been accustomed to; and second, if the owner has been unable to obtain any of the suggested items (and perhaps has not liked to say so), then the puppy will not suffer as a result. Into my starter packs I put puppy milk powder, canned meat, biscuit meal (kibble), breakfast cereal, calcium and vitamin tablets. My diet sheet also contains rearing hints such as where the puppy should sleep, and what to do if it develops diarrhoea. I tell all this to the new owners, but giving it to them in printed form means that anything forgotten in the excitement of the moment may be instantly recalled.

I encourage my puppy owners to ring me as often as they feel the need and some feel this need very often indeed! I believe it is far better that they should ring me for what might seem the most trivial thing than panic and do the wrong thing.

Buying an Adult Dog

If the idea of an older dog appeals to you, remember that he will have become used to the ways of other people by the time you get him and you will have to take him on trust. That is to say, you will have to take as the truth whatever the person who is parting with him tells you. In my experience, when someone is desperate to part with a dog, he will tell you anything, and not always the truth.

In no way do I want to damn the idea of having an adult dog. Up to the present, I have acquired five adult Golden Retrievers at various times. Their ages have varied from eighteen months to six years when they have arrived. All have been quite delightful and have remained with me throughout their lives. I can truthfully say I have never regretted having any of them for a single moment. I do, however, think it is a sensible arrangement to have the dog join you for a trial period. The value of this arrangement is twofold: first, if the dog has some temperament problem, which could make him totally unsuited to your household (unlikely in this breed but possible), this will become apparent; second, the knowledge that you have him on approval eliminates the panic if things go wrong at first and, by the law of averages, some things will.

Remember that adult dogs are parted with for a variety of reasons, some genuine, and some less so. It could be that a breeder is overstocked and must rehouse some adults. It could also happen that an exhibitor has kept two litter-sisters until she has decided which one she wishes to show, making the other available. Two of the more common reasons for a Golden Retriever requiring rehousing are a marriage break up or the owner dying.

There are wonderful rescue organizations, which take in Golden Retrievers of all ages needing homes, and work very hard to place them in permanent, loving homes. Many lovely adults (and youngsters) are available. A list of the good people running these establishments is obtainable from breed clubs (*see* Appendices, page 237).

Dog or Bitch?

Having decided whether a puppy or an adult is what you require, the next decision is whether to have a dog or bitch. In this breed, I can honestly state that both are equally delightful. Many people who contact me make such statements as, 'I don't want a dog because they wander'. My answer to this is that they only wander if you permit it. Incidentally, so do bitches! Another common belief is that bitches are more faithful than dogs. This is not true. Male and female Golden Retrievers are utterly devoted to their families and the males exhibit none of the unpleasant tendencies associated with some breeds.

Male dogs are bigger and heavier. They are also incredibly hand-some and full of fun. Bitches are sweet and gentle and equally full of fun. On the negative side, bitches tend to put on weight more in the middle years and, of course, they do come into season twice yearly. If having an in-season bitch will interfere with your family routine too much, then you would be wise to choose a male. If you have young children who cannot always be relied upon to close doors, steer clear of a bitch until the family is older and more responsible.

Some breeders insure their puppies and adults and hand over the certificate to the new owners. Various insurance companies offer different forms of cover but most will insure against death from injury or illness. Some cover veterinary surgeons' fees. Premiums and types of cover vary, so it is well worth shopping around and comparing what different companies have to offer. If the breeder insures the litter, he will usually hand over a cover note to the new owner, which may be extended or discontinued as that person decides.

Breeders will sometimes issue health certificates for their puppies, but unless a puppy is going abroad, this is not something I do, although, if a new puppy owner asked for one, I would view it as a reasonable request and would comply. I would, however, suggest that after the vet has examined the puppy, it is not returned to its litter-mates but goes straight to its new home. This is to avoid any risk of the vet bringing infection to the rest of the litter.

4

Puppy Management

It is important to prepare for the arrival of your puppy in advance. Ensure that you have the food recommended by the breeder, as any change from what the puppy is accustomed to will result in diarrhoea. If the diet sheet states 'puppy milk', ascertain the exact brand, as there is a wide variety of products available and your aim should be to avoid any change. For the same reason, make sure you know what type of meal has been given.

If he is to sleep in the house, prepare an area that is to be his alone. He should not be where the family must step over him as they pass through the room. An area under a fitted working surface in the kitchen is ideal. This will be warm and out of the way. He may either sleep on a blanket or have a bed of his own with a blanket inside. There are many types of bed available but I would advise you to wait until he is an adult before buying one. There are two reasons for this: the first is that he is almost certain to chew; and the second is that a bed in which he fits snugly when he first arrives will very soon be too small. If you buy an adult-sized bed to begin with, he will feel lost.

At night, the puppy is best confined to a small area rather than having the whole kitchen in which to get lost. A puppy play-pen made of wire mesh is ideal as it can be folded away when not in use. A play-pen will also confine the mess to a smaller area if the puppy relieves itself during the night.

If he is to sleep outside, he will need a small, draught-proof area, preferably inside another building. A small tea-chest is ideal, filled with straw or lined with a thick blanket. Golden Retrievers do not mind cool temperatures as long as they are dry and out of draughts.

Collecting your Puppy

When collecting your puppy, it is a good idea to get someone else to drive you to the kennels so that you will be free to cope with the puppy on the way home. If you do need to go alone, ensure that you have some sort of travelling crate with you to restrain the puppy while you are driving. The wire-mesh type from which it has an uninterrupted view of its surroundings is ideal. I also like the fibreglass carriers, which originated as the best means of conveying dogs by air. They are filled in on three sides, having a mesh door at one end and a ventilated panel at the other. This type is easy to scrub and may be hung on the line to dry.

I think the very best way for a puppy to travel is for it to be held on the owner's lap. This gives it the idea that the experience is totally pleasurable and will get it off to a good start regarding future car travel. A sensible precaution is to cover your lap with a thick towel and have another by your side. I also take a roll of kitchen tissue for mopping up and a large plastic bag in which to place any soiled articles. The better the preparations are, the less likelihood there is of their being needed. Most puppies fall asleep quite quickly and remain that way for the duration of the journey.

On arriving home, it is sensible to take the puppy out to the garden to relieve itself. If it obliges, praise it profusely. If it does not relieve itself, remember that the puppy has no reason to associate this new

From the moment the puppy joins your family, he is learning new things.

Most Golden Retrievers are very bright and soon understand what is required of them.

environment with such a practice as, since birth, it has been used to using other areas.

Next, offer a drink of water or milk. Food should not be offered for at least an hour after the journey. Do not be disappointed if the puppy sniffs its food suspiciously and walks away. It is surrounded by all sorts of exciting things and food will rank low on its list of priorities. Take away the dish (leaving uneaten food down is a bad habit) and offer him a meal later when he has had a chance to explore.

The first day in its new home will probably be the most exhausting of the puppy's life. It is essential for puppies to sleep when they feel tired. Children must be made to understand that puppies are not toys. While they may be played with when *they* feel like it, they need their sleep and should be allowed to remain undisturbed.

From the moment the puppy joins your family, it is learning new things: the puppy is what you make it. Be firm with it but also be patient. It will sometimes disobey because it does not understand, which is very different from being wilfully disobedient. If the need to punish a puppy arises, you have failed miserably. The secret is to stop disobedience *as* it develops. Prevention is truly better than cure.

Golden Retrievers are a most responsive breed and a sharp 'No!' is usually all that is required to stop them in their tracks. If your puppy persists in chewing chair legs, a 'No!' will usually stop it, if only momentarily, when you should give it a toy and praise it. It is important to establish the association of the sharp tone of your voice with the undesirable action, and the pleased tone with correct behaviour. Most Golden Retrievers are very bright and will soon understand.

Diet

All animals appreciate routine and Golden Retrievers are no exception. Meals should be given at set times. An eight-week-old puppy should be having four meals a day and the diet sheet given to you by the breeder should be closely adhered to, the only variation being the quantities, which increase according to the puppy's appetite. In case no such chart is available, the following is an adequate guide:

Diet Sheet for an Eight-Week-Old Puppy

Breakfast 8 a.m.
Cereal and milk (⅓ pint/6 fl. oz), or
scrambled egg, or
wholemeal bread and milk, or
cupful of soaked complete puppy food, or
biscuit meal and milk.

Lunch 12.30 p.m.
Tinned puppy meat (approximately ⅓–½ tin depending on tolerance
   level) with soaked meal, or
white fish and brown bread, or
complete diet, or
cooked minced beef/chicken/rabbit.

Dinner 5 p.m.
Any of the variations given for breakfast.

Supper 9.30 p.m.
Handful of dry biscuit shapes, or
wholemeal toast cut into cubes, with melted cheese, or
cereal and milk again.

Remember that quantities will vary from one individual to another. What is a full meal for one puppy will need to be half as large again for another. If your puppy constantly leaves food in his dish, you are giving him too much, so reduce the quantity. Never leave his dish down if he refuses his food, as this just encourages him to be fussy. He must learn that food that is not eaten is quickly removed. To leave half-eaten food lying around is bad animal husbandry, as well as being most unhygienic.

Some dogs cannot tolerate cow's milk but will tolerate other types. Sometimes a Golden Retriever will exhibit total aversion to milk even if it is disguised in rice pudding or scrambled egg. There are many milk powders available, some closely resembling bitch's milk. The correct dilution of these is critical if maximum benefit is to be obtained. Goat's milk is often tolerated by Golden Retrievers who cannot digest cow's milk. Another advantage of goat's milk is that it freezes successfully.

Over the years, I have had several Golden Retrievers who could not digest eggs. All liked eggs and would eat them with great enthusiasm, but diarrhoea and sickness resulted. Sometimes hard-boiled eggs solved the problem. I once had a complete litter who suffered from diarrhoea as soon as they had eaten eggs.

The type of meat you feed to your puppy is partly dictated by what its breeder has been using, and is also a matter of personal choice. There are several different brands of meat specifically for puppy feeding. There are also tins of tripe, chicken or rabbit, which although not specifically intended for feeding puppies, are eminently suitable.

Chicken and rabbit is good food for puppies and hardly ever upsets them. Cost sometimes makes the feeding of these prohibitive but it is possible to find inexpensive sources, especially if you buy in bulk. The same applies to fish and I have never met a puppy who either did not like fish, or who was upset by it. Fish bones must be removed before feeding and the only certain way to do this is with your fingers.

Beef has always been considered good food but is often too high in price. Butchers sometimes provide what they call 'pet mince' which is the minced off-cuts from joints. If this is not too high in fat content, it is suitable puppy food. It is a good idea to allow this to cool and then skim the fat from the top.

The puppy should have his own food dish, which should be kept as clean as dishes used by the family. A water dish should always be kept full and changed daily. This constant supply of water is vital, especially so if your puppy is fed on a complete food.

A good appetite is generally a sign of good health but there are few, very few Golden Retrievers who just pick at their food for no reason. Such puppies stay very lean and are seldom as contented as their counterparts who regularly eat large quantities. If a puppy who normally eats well suddenly refuses food, the cause must be investigated. If this obvious change in appetite occurs around twelve weeks of age, the fact that the puppy is losing his milk teeth and gaining the permanent ones is often to blame.

Sometimes a puppy merely develops a strong dislike for a food. The only answer is to find something he does like. When all else fails, I have found pilchards are normally readily accepted, as are sardines. Liver, kidney and heart make good food for dogs but are rich so must be fed sparingly. Sometimes liver grated on top of the accustomed food will persuade the puppy to eat it. Grated cheese usually has the same result, and most puppies like cottage cheese.

When to increase quantities becomes obvious as the puppy demands more at each meal. The time to cut down the number of meals is dictated when the puppy picks at a meal. I leave out the midday meal first, then omit the last one each day.

If your puppy stays very lean, it is a good idea to continue to give three meals until there is an improvement in his condition. My lean, show Golden Retrievers stay on three meals until they are two years old. Some of the young males are very slow to body up.

What to add to your puppy's food is a subject which could take many pages without a solution being reached. For years, I added calcium and oil, then in the form of the now frowned-upon cod-liver oil. I believed I was aiding bone formation and adding gloss to the coat. Then I met the Scandinavian Golden Retrievers, who were not given either supplement, and yet they were very glossy and most had excellent hips. Even so, I give a general vitamin supplement tablet to my dogs. As their coats are glossy and their hips are well within the limits of normality for breeding, I consider this to be adequate.

Worming your Puppy

It is vitally important that you ascertain when your puppy was wormed by his breeder (ideally, this should have happened more than once) and that you continue to worm him until there are no obvious signs of infestation.

An owner once said to me that worming was expensive, but it is not half as expensive as feeding the worms indefinitely, which is precisely what the good food given to the puppy will do unless you eradicate the infestation.

Many worm preparations can be bought over the counter, but none is as effective as those obtained from your veterinary surgeon. The choice is wide and the preparation may be in liquid or tablet form. I favour the liquid type, which is administered by mouth, using a syringe with the needle removed. Dosing in this way is quite accurate as there is none of the wastage associated with crushed tablets given in food.

Most worming preparations cause the worms to be expelled from the body. I prefer this type of wormer to one that removes all traces. At least you can see whether the puppy has them or not.

It is important to dose twice, at ten-day intervals. The first dose destroys the worms and the second kills the eggs. It is only by worming in this way that the majority of worms will be destroyed. It is desirable to worm at ten-day intervals until there is no visible sign. After this, worm every six months, or when you see signs.

The presence of worms is nothing to be ashamed of, nor is it a sign that the breeder was negligent. Some litters show very little sign of infestation whereas others are positively riddled with them. I always give to the new owners the wormer that the puppies have been used to. This ensures that the treatment is continued.

Vaccinations

It is of the utmost importance that your puppy completes a course of vaccination against the killer diseases: distemper, leptospirosis, hepatitis and parvovirus. If he is not fully protected and comes into contact with these diseases, he will have no resistance to the infection and will most probably die.

Some breeders start the vaccination programme as early as six weeks. As puppies retain much of their maternal immunity at this stage, I have never followed this programme and prefer to wait until twelve weeks. If I lived in a high risk area (I live in an isolated spot, well away from roads or neighbours), I would act differently.

It is vitally important that your puppy is confined to your premises until his course of vaccination is completed. You must not take him out, nor must you permit other dogs to come into contact with him. I am so paranoid about the possibility of infection that I positively discourage visitors at this stage and any who come are requested to wear my kennel boots! I would sooner risk being labelled a fanatic than risk the life of a single puppy.

Consult your vet before you collect your puppy and find out what vaccination programme he advises. My vet vaccinates at twelve and sixteen weeks and I request a booster before the puppy goes to its first show. If you are still anxious, a single blood test will reveal the level of immunity. This is the only positive way of ascertaining whether or not your puppy is at risk.

Confining your puppy to your own house and garden has a detrimental effect on its socialization but there is still much you can do to accustom it to the world at large. During this isolation period, it can be introduced to household sounds such as the vacuum cleaner and washing machine. Radio and television provide many unexpected noises, so are invaluable instruments of training. Also, there is no reason why your puppy cannot make short journeys in its

Confining your puppy to his own garden is essential until all his vaccinations are completed. This beautiful 8-week-old puppy grew up to be Sh.Ch. Camrose Tulfes Intirol.

travelling box in order to accustom it to your car. Time spent in this way pays dividends later on.

Early Training

Most Golden Retrievers can be house-trained very easily and if carried outside as soon as they wake or finish a meal they will most certainly oblige. At night, thick newspaper placed away from the blanket will usually be instantly identified by your puppy as the toilet area. Praise the puppy enthusiastically when it uses it.

Remember that puppies, like small babies, are unable to control their bladders at night. If they feel the need to relieve themselves, they respond, irrespective of where they are. I find male puppies take longer to be dry all night than females. Puppies find it more difficult to last all night during cold weather. By five months, most Golden Retrievers are clean all night but, obviously, there are exceptions and also the occasional lapses.

Training your puppy to the collar and lead is dealt with more fully in Chapter 6 (see page 101), but it is valuable practice to try ten minutes walking on a collar and lead daily from about twelve weeks old. A lightweight collar and lead should be used. The collars which are part nylon webbing and part chain are ideal. An ordinary collar needs to be too tight for comfort if it is to be tight enough to prevent the puppy jerking his head free. On a main road, this could have tragic consequences. Collars of nylon and chain tighten when the puppy pulls and release when he stops. They are far kinder than the check chain, which I would never consider using on a puppy.

Your puppy should wear a light collar for a short period each day. Never leave a puppy unattended with its collar on as it could become entangled in something, with tragic results. The longer you leave training your puppy to the collar and lead, the more adverse its reaction is likely to be. If a collar is fitted when the puppy is young, it is less likely to be aware of it.

When children are introduced to your puppy, insist that they sit down, preferably on the floor. Puppies can be perfectly still one moment and then fling themselves backwards without warning. If the child is on the floor and a puppy does this, the results will be minimal. If the same thing occurs when the child is on a chair, or standing, there could be dire results. Teach the child to talk to the puppy and stroke it gently in the direction the hair lies.

Puppies who are teething chew anything and that includes fingers, chins, toes and earlobes! Explain to the child that this is not a sign of aggression but of affection. A favourite toy will usually distract the puppy and occupy his teeth!

Introducing other canine members of your family to a new puppy needs to be handled tactfully. Allow them to meet it one at a time and let the puppy be on the floor for the meeting. Golden Retrievers usually accept puppies with little fuss but occasionally one will view the newcomer with disgust. Your role is to take the heat out of the situation. Do not permit puppy and adult to enter into any sort of confrontation. A walk around the garden with the two will often lead the older one to accept the puppy more quickly.

Areas to watch carefully are when your adults are feeding or sleeping. Your puppy will not understand that it must not rush into your stud dog's dinner, so should be put in a position where this cannot happen. Put him outside or in his play-pen or cage at feeding time. This will prevent a potentially difficult situation from developing. Having said this, I have known very few Golden Retrievers who were not completely tolerant of puppies.

Similarly, do not permit your puppy to jump on to a sleeping adult. Your dog could be startled and snap before he is fully awake. With care, such situations need never arise.

Never leave a new puppy alone with adult dogs or cats until you have supervised their relationship for quite a while. If you are present, many potentially unpleasant situations can be averted. If you are not there, anything might happen.

Finally, enjoy your puppy. Do not allow the anxiety of owning a dog to burden you to the degree where worry displaces pleasure. There is so much fun to be had from watching a puppy grow and it would be a pity if you did not enjoy it to the full.

5

Adolescent and Adult Management

The transition from puppy to young adult is a gradual process and there is no specific moment when this takes place. Technically, your Golden Retriever ceases to be classed as a puppy when he is one year old but some act like puppies all their lives.

Once he reaches this age, it is time to think about having his eyes examined by a qualified ophthalmologist. Even if you are not going to show your dog or use him for breeding, it is satisfying for you to know that he has no inherited eye defects and this information will be gratefully received by the breeder. How to arrange for an eye test is dealt with in Chapter 10 (*see* page 179).

Camrose Fabius Tarquin (later Ch.) at just 9 months old showing all the promise which was eventually fulfilled.

It is also advisable to think about making an appointment to have his hips X-rayed (*see* Chapter 10, pages 180–6). I usually have my dogs X-rayed at around fifteen months old. Other breeders prefer them to be younger and some leave it as late as eighteen months.

When your puppy becomes adolescent, he will most likely pass through the leggy stage where he appears to be all head and very little body. Gone will be the attractive puppy roundness. If he is a good eater, this stage will only be temporary. If he is not such a good eater, this stage lasts longer. Some Golden Retrievers are very slow to mature anyway and one who picks at his food is likely to take even longer.

Diet

The best way to feed a Golden Retriever is a matter of very individual opinion. The choice of dog food is enormous. If you talk to a dozen breeders you will most likely be given twelve sets of contrasting advice. My advice is to find a diet that suits your dog, and stick with it. Dogs do not need the variety so liked by humans, in fact, too much variety tends to upset them.

Often a Golden Retriever's feeding pattern is set by his breeder. The new owners continue to use the food he was reared on, then contact the breeder for advice (if they have not been given an adult diet sheet) on how to continue feeding into adulthood.

The time to alter the diet is when, for no apparent reason, as sometimes happens, a Golden Retriever goes off food that he has previously eaten with enthusiasm. As long as you are able to ascertain that this aversion to the usual food is not a result of poor health, it is time to try something else.

There is a bewildering amount of various foodstuffs available. You will find many 'complete' or 'balanced' foods offered. These are foods which need no additions (except water in some cases), and have the correct balance of protein and all the other nutrients needed by the growing dog. Read the instructions carefully as some are geared for feeding at certain stages or during pregnancy or old age. Do not imagine you will do your Golden Retriever any good by feeding him one of the very high protein foods intended for Greyhounds, as this is not the case.

These foods vary a great deal in appearance and some may be composed entirely of flaked ingredients, whilst others are pelleted like so much of the food fed to farm stock. Some are mixtures of pellets and flakes. Others are crunchy.

The advantage of giving complete foods is that they remove the guesswork from feeding. You can rest assured your dog's diet is balanced. Such foods are also very clean to handle and exceptionally easy to prepare. Sometimes the quantities per meal suggested on the bags are rather generous. Be guided by your dog's condition, or obvious lack of it.

The disadvantage of feeding a complete diet is that some Golden Retrievers simply do not like it. Also a dog fed on such foods will excrete a larger volume of waste than dogs fed on meat and biscuits. If disposing of waste matter is a problem where you live, this is a point well worth considering. Dogs fed in this way tend to drink large quantities of water, which must be available at all times. Obviously, the intake of such volume leads to the production of more urine. All these points are worth thinking about if you are the one who does the clearing up.

The alternative to feeding complete foods is to feed meat (either tinned, fresh or dried), and biscuit. The choice of tinned meat is wide. Look at the protein content. Some are surprisingly low, yet are not low priced. Some Golden Retrievers cannot tolerate tinned meat and diarrhoea is the result. If your Golden Retriever reacts in this way you will have to resign yourself to feeding him in a different way. Most dogs like dried meat. It is clean to handle, smells appetizing and will soak if you prefer not to give it dry. My dogs have dried meat and will do anything to get into the chest where it is stored. I obtain my supply from a dripping manufacturer, and so I am sure it is fit for human consumption.

If you feed raw meat, be absolutely certain of the safety of your source. Never buy from a fell monger (one who deals with fallen stock), as it is impossible to tell what the animal died from. I remember one lovely litter dying as a result of eating contaminated meat. The only safe way to feed raw meat is to buy it from a butcher but, for most, the price is prohibitive.

Many dogs enjoy a meal of tripe. I have to say I do not feed tripe to my dogs because I simply cannot bear the smell when it is cooking. By tripe I do not mean the cream-coloured variety that comes from a butcher, but the green type obtained from the abattoir. If you have not experienced the smell, I can only say it will exceed your imagination. Should you decide to obtain some and, for safety's sake, cook it, be warned! Many dogs who cannot tolerate other tinned meats will cope well with tinned chicken or tripe, or a mixture of both. I find these seldom upset Golden Retrievers.

Biscuit needs to be fed in addition to meat; it may be meal or whole, dry biscuit. Again, it is worth shopping around when choosing biscuits as there is a vast difference in the prices of some brands. Some brands having a very similar analysis will have a totally dissimilar price, and the most expensive brand is not necessarily the best.

Biscuit meal may be soaked and mixed with whatever type of meat you use, or it can be used dry. Some Golden Retrievers will only eat dry meal and exhibit something approaching nausea if offered soaked meal. Do remember that dry meal swells to more than double its size in the stomach. If dogs will accept soaked meal I prefer to feed it this way, so prevent greedy dogs from eating large quantities dry, then drinking water and causing it to swell.

Yet another way of feeding is to give meat and biscuit at separate meals. The biscuit may be given in cake or shapes form. Most Golden Retrievers love hard biscuit to chew. Again, there are others who will never eat any form of hard biscuit. I have an otherwise greedy bitch who backs away from her dish if I offer her any form of hard, dry, biscuit.

If meat and biscuit is fed, some owners feel the need to add oil, usually the vegetable variety. It certainly imparts a good gloss to the coat. There are all sorts of proprietary brands of vitamin and mineral tablets which, if the sales figures are accurate, are extremely popular.

The following feeding regime is the one I use for my non-pregnant adult dogs: I give hard biscuits to chew at breakfast-time (the quantity varies according to the age and condition of the dog – the young dogs and bitches having considerably more than anyone else); the old dogs have fine biscuit meal with milk; each is given a chunk of dried meat to chew. At tea-time all have meat and biscuit-meal. Some have tinned meat and those who cannot tolerate this, eat dried meat. I add oil of primrose in capsule form to the dishes of the dogs I am showing. The diet I give to my in-whelp and nursing bitches is outlined in Chapter 9.

There is no mystique to dog feeding. Good food makes good dogs, and there is no cheap way of feeding animals, which will give the desired results. But it is possible to go to the other extreme: there is no evidence to show that dogs do better on best steak than they do on meat intended for feeding to dogs.

Exercise

Much has been written about exercising dogs. Quite often, the recommended distances to be walked in order to ensure sufficient exercise are beyond the bounds of possibility: I have never met anyone who walked such vast distances on a regular basis. However, Golden Retrievers are active dogs whose size and character demand daily exercise consisting of more than a short walk round a small back garden.

My dogs are free all day and spend a lot of time chasing one another. They also have regular exercise in the forest, where they dash about until they reach the state where they cannot manage more than an orderly walk back to the car.

Some people believe in restricting the exercise of young puppies but I do not agree that this is of any benefit. Mine are free to run and play all day. They are also free to sleep when they choose, which I feel is very important. I do not, however, take my puppies for organized exercise until they are over six months old.

I frequently read that regular roadwork keeps nails short, but I have never seen evidence of this. I believe some Golden Retrievers have long nails however they are exercised. Mine are exercised on grass, yet hardly ever need to have their nails trimmed. For road work to be of any real benefit, it would have to be too punishing for most owners.

Housing

You will have to decide where your dog is going to live. I hope you have decided that he will be part of the family, as this is how Golden Retrievers like to live. Mine (all fifteen of them) potter about all day in the paddock and in the farmyard. When the cows are being fed, they help. If fencing or gates are being repaired, they supervise that too. Whatever you do, they are there, doing it with you.

Even if you own one Golden Retriever who is to be a house dog, he will need a place of his own where he is not disturbed and from where he cannot disturb you. Some owners favour the wire-mesh or fibreglass travelling crate as a sleeping place. Personally, I have never become accustomed to seeing a little golden face imprisoned.

Most houses have an area outside which could become a kennel. Sometimes there is the possibility of converting an outhouse for the purpose, but, if you do this, remember that heat rises and, if your dog is to be warm, he will need some sort of box with a top on it to sleep in to conserve his body heat.

Ideally, your night-time arrangements for your puppy and adolescent dog will be a warm bed with a furry blanket. You will also need a small night-time run so that he can relieve himself without soiling his bed. A concrete run with newspaper or sawdust in one corner is ideal. Golden Retrievers are naturally clean and hate to soil their beds.

If you are embarking upon the erection of kennels, this venture needs a lot of thought. Kennels are very expensive and I have yet to meet the Golden Retriever who is not capable of reducing wooden buildings to matchsticks! Any wooden beds in my kennels are edged with steel sheeting and all wooden doors are lined with it. This defeats the most enthusiastic chewers.

Brick or breeze-block kennels are dearer at the outset, but the cheapest in the long term. The same goes for steel-bar fencing. My dogs have reduced even the thickest gauge chain-link to mere strands and they really love the plastic coated variety, which they strip in minutes. Heavy-gauge square mesh is preferable to chain-link but needs to be heavy and the squares need to be small (especially for puppies who manage to get their lower jaws stuck through the larger mesh, their teeth preventing withdrawal without assistance).

My kennel block exists as a place to contain dogs when the need arises. They spend all their days running free but the kennel doors are open so that they can put themselves to bed if they choose. I favour the idea of a pop-hole in the kennel doors, as this allows the dogs free access but cuts down on draughts. There is no heating in my adults' kennels yet they always feel warm and seem comfortable.

If your dogs are going to spend some time in their kennels and runs, the exercise area should be large enough to allow them to play. I have seen runs in kennels which vary in size from a tennis court to a chicken-run. The surface of the run should be concrete, sloping slightly towards a drain to facilitate easy draining after scrubbing. When the concrete is laid, it is a good idea to have a brushed finish rather than a perfectly smooth one. This enables dogs to have a good grip of the surface, especially in wet conditions.

Some people use coke cinders as a floor covering, but I find it hard to believe that any dog would feel comfortable running over such a surface. Also, I cannot imagine the state of the dogs' coats that are in constant contact with cinders, nor can I imagine cleaning out such a run.

I find a concrete surface tends to go green with age but one of the garden-path washes to prevent this formation of algae will put a stop to this. Read the instructions carefully and dilute accurately, not allowing the dogs to return to their run until it is dry. An algae-coated surface is very slippery and is a menace to human and canine feet.

The choice of bedding in kennels is a matter of personal taste. My preference is for the veterinary, fleecy fabric that is now widely available. The drawback with this is that puppies (and some older Golden Retrievers) like to play tug-of-war with it, so reducing it to a bedraggled mess. It is possible to lessen the chance of this occurring by removing the bedding during the day, or by denying them access to the sleeping areas.

Many kennels use straw in winter and bare boards in summer. There are several types of straw and some are more liable to insect infestation than others. I find barley straw particularly itch-causing, both to those handling it and to the dogs. Wheat straw is only a little better. Oat straw is the clean, bright golden type, often more difficult to obtain but by far the best. It is the one favoured by racehorse studs. If straw is used, a rigorous routine of discarding and replacing it regularly should be observed. In use, straw becomes broken and dusty and I cannot believe the inhalation of such dust is anything but harmful.

A word of warning about the use of straw: nowadays, many crops are sprayed, so try to find out what your straw was treated with and, if possible, try to obtain your supply from a place where no sprays are used. On a purely practical note, remember that straw is highly inflammable. I do not allow smoking anywhere near my kennel.

I have seen shredded paper used as bedding and those using it seem well pleased with the results. I tried a sample bale, but did not like it at all. The shreds of paper clung to the feathering of the dogs and, consequently, were distributed over a wide area. If you do decide on shredded paper, ensure it is the white variety, as shredded newspaper leaves an inky residue on damp dogs.

Many kennels favour wood-shavings for bedding. Whilst I like the fresh smell of shavings, I dislike them for the same reasons that I dislike paper: they attach themselves to feathering and are spread over a wide area. On a more serious note, there is the risk that puppies may choke on shavings.

I am aware that boarding and quarantine kennels hose runs daily, but I am not in favour of this. My runs are used so rarely and soiled even less frequently, that it is sufficient to brush them out regularly, remove any soiling and scrub the affected spot. When the whole runs need washing, there is nothing better than hot, diluted household bleach. Obviously the dogs must be absent when this is being done and must not return until the area is completely dry. Take great care to ensure no residual bleach lurks in runnels or drains. Since Golden Retrievers have a need to taste most things they encounter, the consequences would be disastrous.

Grooming

Care of the Golden Retriever's coat is as simple or complex as you choose to make it. If your Golden Retriever is a pet, he needs to be kept clean, neat and tangle-free. This will necessitate the occasional bath and regular brushing and combing.

Bathing

Bathing a pet dog needs to be done when his coat lacks its usual gloss or when he smells less than fresh. Golden Retrievers are remarkably free from the odour that affects some breeds but, in old age, they tend to take on a stronger smell than in youth. I always bath my bitches after they have finished their season. This not only cleans any fur, which may have become soiled, but removes the trace of any odour which might attract unwelcome attention from male dogs.

Where you bath your Golden Retriever is a matter of personal choice. I find bending over a bath quite exhausting and, if there are several dogs to be bathed, it is nearly impossible to straighten up when you have completed the task. A bath also has the disadvantage of being steep-sided, necessitating the lifting of the dog in and out, which is not easy with a fully grown male, nor with a squirming puppy.

The arrangements I find most convenient, and to which the dogs adapt surprisingly quickly, is a raised shower tray, so that the dogs are about 2 feet (60cm) off the ground. The hand-held shower attachment needs to be wall mounted, behind the dog. A fixed shower makes it virtually impossible to direct the water when rinsing.

There is no mystique about shampooing a dog. First, stand him in the tray or bath and wet his coat thoroughly. Then, work the shampoo into a lather, starting from the head and moving down to the tail, making sure that you soap the long hair on the backs of the legs and the tail. I generally use an insecticidal shampoo, which can be bought over the counter, but if the dogs are scratching or biting at their fur, so suggesting parasites, I obtain a stronger preparation from my veterinary surgeon.

Leave the shampoo on for three or four minutes and then rinse thoroughly. The thoroughness of the rinsing is of great importance as shampoo remaining in the coat dulls it and causes irritation. Pay particular attention to the underside of the dog and inside the legs where the shampoo collects.

Drying a dog is easier with a hair-drier, but some dogs simply will not tolerate this. Most of mine accept this method quite happily but the odd one will scoot away as soon as the appliance appears! Even if you do use a drier, the dog needs to be towelled first to remove the excess water. Dogs who refuse to stand while a hair drier is used will have to be completely towel-dried.

If your dog is being shown, he will need a bath before most shows, particularly if he is pale. If he has a profuse coat he will need to be bathed one or two full days before the show in order to allow his coat to settle and to permit the return of some of the natural oil, which is responsible for the gloss. I direct the hair-drier with one hand, and brush the coat flat with the other. With profusely coated dogs it is beneficial to wrap something fine, like a net curtain around them as they lie down. Some breeders use a T-shirt but I have never managed this very successfully: as fast as I fit it on, my dogs are struggling to remove it!

Clean the ears after a bath. Do not fall into the trap of using ear drops if your dog is to be shown the following day. I have often come across exhibits with greasy fur on the insides of their ears and on their necks as a result of recent ear cleaning. After bathing, clean the visible parts of the ear, including the flap, with cotton wool moistened with warm water and dipped in a weak solution of diluted shampoo. Rinse it with wet cotton wool and then towel dry. Do not allow water to enter the ear canal, and never probe into the ear.

Dry preparations are available for cleaning the coat but I have never been impressed by them. However well one brushes, there is always enough residue to dull the coat. It takes as long to dry-clean as it does to bath and the results of bathing are far preferable. Of

Trimmed head in close-up.

course, dry-cleaning would be very advantageous with old or rheumatic dogs.

Trimming

The show Golden Retriever needs regular trimming to enhance his outline. Trimming will not change a poor-quality dog into a good one, but it will make a good one a great deal better. Whether you trim before or after bathing your dog is a matter of personal choice. I trim before bathing as I find the coat looks less newly trimmed this way.

To trim successfully, it is essential to have a practical demonstration. If you have a local dog club, you might like to suggest that they organize a trimming session. Failing this, there is nothing to stop a group of Golden Retriever enthusiasts getting together and inviting an experienced exhibitor to give a demonstration.

The best sort of session involves the trimming demonstration followed by an opportunity for the audience to have a go at trimming their own dogs. I always suggest that the side facing away from the judge is trimmed first. Then, if mistakes are made, they are not instantly obvious.

The secret of successful trimming is to remove very little hair at a time and then to comb so that you can monitor the effect. Remember, you can always take more off but you cannot replace any removed in error.

Start by brushing and combing the dog all over, paying particular

A group of immaculately presented Golden Retrievers belonging to the famous Dewmist Kennel owned by Henric Fryckstrand, Sweden. (Photo Fryckstrand)

Untrimmed Golden Retriever.

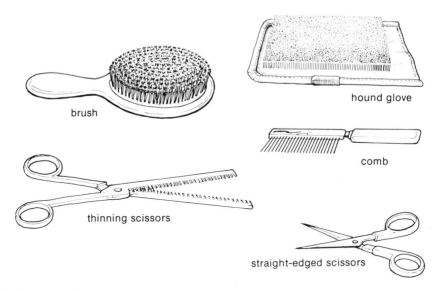

Trimming equipment.

attention to the feathering on the backs of the legs and on the tail. Two types of scissors are needed for trimming: thinning scissors with 32 teeth, (this is important as more teeth render the scissors too fine and fewer, too coarse). I find those made of blue steel last longer and stay sharper, although they are more costly. The other pair you will need is the short, sharp type favoured by hairdressers.

Begin trimming the neck underneath the lower jaw with the thinning scissors. Work upwards, against the natural direction of the hair, pushing the thinning scissors underneath the hair near the roots. Make no more than three cuts before combing the hair to observe the effect. Never cut across the hair or steps will result, which take months to grow out. This thinning process is carried out over the whole chest. The idea is to neaten the profile of the dog and to accentuate the shape. He should not look as if he has been shaved. In the USA this chest hair is left much longer than it is in Britain.

Next, give the dog a rest by getting him to lie on his side. With the straight-edged scissors, remove the excess hair from around the pads. I also cut straight up the edge of the pastern to the stopper pad to neaten the ragged fur. Golden Retrievers often have knots between their toes and you should regularly examine this area and trim off any offending tufts. It can be very painful for a dog to have

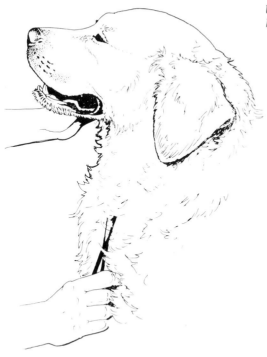

Use thinning scissors to reduce hair on chest.

knotted hair between his toes and, if it is not removed, it can cause a sore patch to form.

While the dog is on his side, trim off any straggly hair that has grown too long below the line of feathering under his body. I also brush the feathering away from the forelegs and trim the very ends of this with straight scissors, leaving it long near the body and shorter at the top of the pastern.

At this stage, the tail is trimmed. Naturally, Golden Retrievers grow a tremendous amount of hair on their tails, often resembling the huge Rough Collie tail. Again, begin by brushing the hair away from the tail, so that it spreads in a fan shape. The finished shape should resemble a cook's knife, longer at the base of the tail, shorter at the tip with a rounded-off point. Do not lean on the tail as you trim, as the dog's automatic reaction is to pull his tail out of your grasp, so making your task doubly difficult. Having trimmed the full length once, comb the hair, then shake it and comb again. It is surprising how many long, straggly hairs which escaped the first trimming become obvious at this stage. Sometimes I need to trim

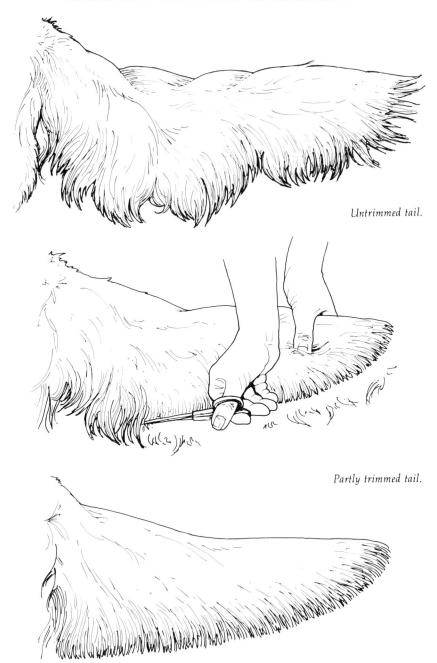

Untrimmed tail.

Partly trimmed tail.

Finished tail.

and shake three or four times before all the hairs have been dealt with. It is arguable how long the tail hair should be at its longest point. Some people like it to be 4 inches (10cm) but I like it a little longer. The only way to know which is the correct length for your dog is to decide whether or not the tail looks in proportion to the rest of his body when he stands up. The end of the tail bone is grasped between the finger and thumb and the rounded-point is formed just beyond this. If your dog has a very short tail, this end needs to be further away from the actual tip. The trimmed tip should reach the top of the hocks.

The hair on the hocks needs to be trimmed off using the thinning scissors. In Scandinavia, this hair is frequently left on and accentuated by brushing and fluffing it outwards, so giving the dog the appearance of having thicker legs than he actually has. I found this very difficult to get used to when I first judged there.

Finish the trimming session by doing the ears, but if the dog is fidgeting and has obviously had enough for one day, this can be left until the next day. The ears grow a lot of hair on the flaps and where they join the head, and all this needs to be neatened. Use the thinning

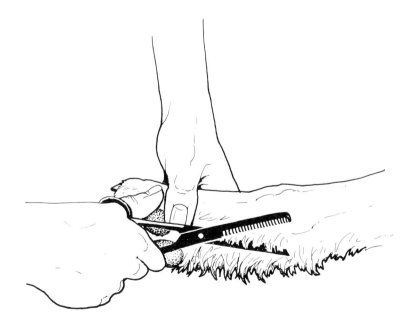

Hair trimmed on back of hocks using thinning scissors.

Thinning hair above the hock.

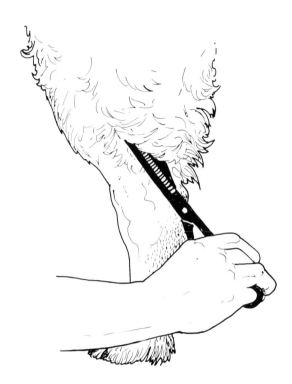

scissors, pushing upwards into the hair, and again using only two or three cuts before combing and assessing what you have done. Remember, you are aiming for a neat and not a barbered appearance. Trim around the very edges with the straight-edged scissors. Take care not to slice into the fur too deeply so that you leave furrows. A natural appearance is desirable so you only want to take off the ends of the hair. When trimming the inside of the ear, where it joins the head, be careful to observe the double flap of skin on the ear edge. It is so easy to catch this with the scissors and once you do this, you will find the dog most reluctant to allow you to trim him in future. The hair behind the ears should be trimmed very close indeed with the scissors.

When trimming, your movements should be gentle and unhurried, and you should attempt to carry an air of confidence (even if this is the last thing you feel) at all times. A dog who is frightened of being trimmed at an early age is very difficult to deal with. I trim my puppies from about five months, even when there is very little to trim, in order to accustom them to the sound of the scissors and to train them to stand still when required.

Use thinning scissors on top of ear.

Neaten the edges with straight scissors.

Trim the hair close behind the ear with thinning scissors.

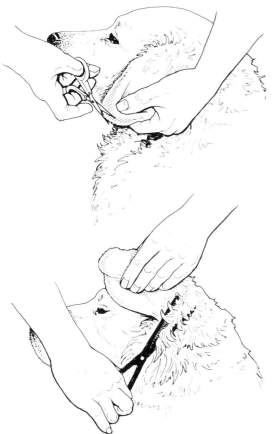

In general, Golden Retrievers love any sort of attention and almost all of them view trimming as extra attention.

Dark-coloured Golden Retrievers are more difficult to trim than pale ones, as any accidental removal of the top coat results in the paler undercoat becoming visible. Ideally, you should practise on a dog you are not going to show, or perhaps a friend will allow you to trim his. Failing that, remember the rule of trimming the side away from the judge first.

One idea which works is to trim your dog in front of a long mirror. You then see what the judge sees. As you become more adept at trimming, you will learn several tricks. You will learn how a patch of slightly longer hair over the breast bone creates the illusion that the angulation of the upper arm is better than it is. I stress that it is an illusion, since no judge worth his salt would be deceived by such artifice, but it is worth trying!

The best way to keep your dog looking immaculate is to trim little and often. It is so easy to do the little bits of trimming as they are

Use thinning scissors on the shoulders, taking care not to remove the top coat.

Trimmed dog.

needed and far less tiring than trimming several show dogs from scratch.

I am sometimes asked if it is necessary to trim Golden Retrievers that are not intended for show. I think they all look, and probably feel, better for being trimmed. In hot weather a good trim is undeniably beneficial.

During the trimming session, check the length of your dog's nails. If necessary, the nails can be clipped using nail clippers designed for dogs, obtainable from good pet shops. Remember that the nails have a quick, a sensitive core possessing the blood supply. It is very painful if you cut this and will bleed profusely. It will also make the dog very wary of having his nails clipped in future. It is seldom necessary to take off more than the very tip, although dew-claws sometimes grow to a good length in older dogs. If you are unhappy about nail-cutting, ask an experienced friend or a veterinary surgeon to do it for you. Most Golden Retrievers never need their nails cut until they get old. Some have the problem that the quick inside the nail reaches almost to the tip, so making any but the slightest trimming very difficult.

Some dogs have very dirty teeth and need to have them scaled. It is possible to do it yourself but, like many Golden Retriever owners, I prefer to let the vet take care of this. Some still scrape away the tartar but others use an ultra-sound device which emits a blue light. The dog is totally unaware of the exercise.

✓ There are several types and flavours of dog toothpastes available. People who use them regularly tell me that their dogs exhibit no aversion to this practice. The secret is probably to accustom them to having their teeth brushed from a very early age; when I tried mine, they struggled a lot and blew bubbles!

Care of the Old Dog

Golden Retrievers remain youthful for many years, possibly longer than any other breed I can name. With some, the ageing process is so gradual that you are hardly aware of it. Others seem to age over-night, which makes it difficult for the owner to adjust.

What are the expected symptoms of old age? Some old dogs still continue to take regular exercise but become stiff as a result. This stiffness manifests itself after a period of rest and the dog has difficulty in rising. I believe it is a mistake to deprive the dog of exercise for as long as he wants to go but in no way should he be forced to. The best idea is to return home before he gets tired, because if you wait until he is lagging behind, he is going to be exhausted by the time you reach home.

Most Golden Retrievers love to swim and have no natural reserve about plunging into ice-cold rivers and lakes. I allow them to continue this for as long as they choose but ensure they are towelled and then dried with a hair-drier on their return. I subscribe to the view that if, by being permitted to participate in something they enjoy so much their life is shortened a little, then so be it. I believe this is the choice they would make for themselves. We have all seen dogs being over-cosseted with the result that they become prematurely old.

The Older Dog's Diet

I find that the old Golden Retriever often needs a different diet from the one he has formerly enjoyed. He is less active and will probably eat less. If you have given one large meal until this time, it is a good idea to divide it into two or three smaller ones. His digestive system will be less effective as he gets older and he will benefit from not having to cope with a single, large mass of food. If his teeth are not good you will also need to alter the consistency of his food. Dogs who have crunched hard biscuits and pelleted diets will be more comfortable with softer food, although I do not advocate feeding a sloppy diet suited to invalids.

Grooming

Ears frequently need more attention in the older dog. It is good practice to have a regular ear-cleaning session with dogs of all ages, but dogs of ten years and over seem to have dirtier ears than younger ones. I use a proprietary ear-cleaner as a matter of routine. Two drops in each ear is sufficient. If there is any sign of infection (characterized by a strong smell and skin which is hot to the touch), this cleaning should be followed with the removal of the matter that comes to the surface and then antibiotic drops should be administered. Any excess lotion should be wiped free from the externally visible part of the ear. If the condition persists, do return to your vet as Golden Retrievers are prone to ear problems and those not cleared quickly can be quite troublesome.

Grooming of the old dog needs to be a regular exercise. My dogs have profuse coats in their youth, which become twice as dense in old age. For some owners, this increased coat is quite a problem. Ten minutes spent brushing and combing each day is a certain way of preventing tangles and matts forming. If you have allowed your old dog to remain ungroomed for quite a while there are several courses of action open to you.

Professional groomers will completely strip out a dog. This is the kindest method of dealing with a dog who has become really matted. If it sounds extreme, I have rescued various unwanted Golden Retrievers over the years, whose coats have been so matted that to try to groom out the knots would have been tantamout to cruelty. Dense matts have a habit of forming in tender areas: behind ears, between the legs and under the tail. I have found some dogs with hair so matted around the testicles and across the anus that the discomfort must have been indescribable. It says much for this lovely breed that these dogs, to whom I am a total stranger, have submitted to my cutting and clipping without the slightest objection.

It is possible for you to tidy up a neglected coat with electric clippers. They are remarkably easy to use (try them on an old piece of fur fabric first if you feel nervous). The disadvantage is that they buzz like an electric shaver and some dogs object. I have clipped my pensioners for years. I do them at the end of spring and in the middle of summer. They might look odd but I am convinced they are twice as comfortable as their unclipped companions. Another thing that clipping does is to make the hair grow really luxuriantly.

Eyes often need attention as they tend to water more frequently in old dogs. This is particularly obvious on a cold or windy day. Eye drops usually give relief and the tear-stained area can be cleaned with cotton wool.

The eyes of old dogs frequently take on a bluish tinge. This should not be confused with hereditary eye problems and is usually just part of growing old. The sight is not necessarily impaired by this bluing: one of my fourteen year olds with very opaque looking eyes can still spot a cat at 100 yards and, even more remarkably, will only attempt to chase if it is not one of ours!

The teeth of old dogs can be a problem. Some become loose, or so covered with tartar, that they are best removed. Extraction requires a general anaesthetic and, while there is always a slight risk with any form of anaesthesia, it should be borne in mind that modern techniques are excellent and the risk is minimal.

Elderly Golden Retrievers deserve to spend their final years in the comfort of the house, even if they have been kennelled all their lives. Suitable beds will be low sided and filled with a fleecy rug in winter. My dogs love to be as near the radiator as possible and old Sh.Ch. Janville Tempestuous liked to sleep on his back with his side pressed against the warmth. Beds with built-in, underfloor heating pads are excellent for arthritic dogs and give much comfort.

Euthanasia

Of all the decisions confronting the dog owner, the hardest one to make is when to part with the old, ailing, dog. Personally, I make this decision when the dog's quality of life is greatly impaired. To keep a dog beyond this point is to indulge yourself; it does not help your dog. It is never an easy decision and, even when I am certain it is the correct thing to do, I still have to ask my vet, 'If he was your dog, what would you do?' I know the answer before I ask the question, but I need the reassurance of someone who knows.

Most of us have, at some time, kept a dog for longer than was in that animal's interest. Often this is because we are frightened of being too hasty, knowing that there is no going back. Also, we are uncertain of what the procedure of parting with a dog entails. Dogs are put to sleep by a single injection. The dog feels no more than if he were being vaccinated. As the injection is administered, the dog becomes drowsy and by the time the needle is withdrawn, it is all over.

If I make this sound easy, let me say that I have cried over all the dogs I have had put to sleep. Sometimes I have walked or driven for hours. Even when I have known it is the only kind solution, it is still a most upsetting experience. It is obvious that if you have loved a dog in life, your suffering at his death will be acute.

In some countries, counselling services are available to those who have lost a pet. When Linchael Wild Cherry died of leukaemia at three years old, she was nursing a litter. I found her death impossible to cope with. I have been upset by the deaths of other dogs but had never experienced total devastation before. I was full of self-recrimination: if only I had not mated her. Had I lost a relative, colleagues would have been totally supportive; but it was 'only a dog'. I clearly remember driving to work the next day, feeling totally unable to cope, and driving off into the country for the day. The grief at losing a much-loved dog is as real as it is at losing a relative. We need to grieve and it is healthy to do so. Even now, I still have to fight against the emotion when I come across Cherry's photographs, and even more when I garden near her grave. I take consolation from having her sisters, Silk and Orchid, but their expressions make me catch my breath on occasions.

Sentimental claptrap? Not at all. I am certain that many reading this will know exactly how I felt. I hope that knowing they are not alone will help others to cope when the occasion presents itself.

6

Training

There are so many excellent books on training for field trials that to compete with them, even if I were able, in the space of a chapter would be impossible. I hope this will serve as a guide to the complete novice who wishes to give his Golden Retriever some basic obedience training, so that he might be a more biddable companion, and also some elementary training with the gun to enable him to run for his Show Gundog Qualifying Certificate.

I must make it quite clear that I do not consider myself an expert in obedience or gundog training. I am aware that there are many tried and tested methods, but I have outlined those I use. It is worth adding that nothing I have done with the dogs has given me so much pleasure as training Ch. Linchael Wild Silk for her qualifier. The training we did was absolutely from scratch, and she was four years old when I entered and qualified her. To those who would like to qualify a Golden Retriever, I can say quite truthfully that if I can do it, anyone can.

Ideally, training any dog begins much earlier than at four years of age. From the time your Golden Retriever leaves the nest, he should regard coming to you as a pleasurable experience and should understand that human hands are for stroking and signalling. There should never be any association with your hands which is anything but pleasurable.

As soon as your Golden Retriever knows his name, make a point of calling him to you and, when he comes, praising him profusely and patting him. Make sure you make a point of calling him when you are not wanting to put him either on the lead or in his kennel. Call him many times, just to praise and occasionally reward with a titbit.

Any serious training should be delayed until after six months but there are several basic rules which your puppy may learn before then. Although I leave formal training as late as possible, I am fully aware that every moment of contact with the puppy reinforces behaviour, both desirable and undesirable. It is this awareness from early on in your puppy's development that sets the pattern for later.

Obedience classes are excellent places for older puppies, once all their vaccinations have been completed. Their benefit is two-fold: not only does the puppy learn to be obedient, but he also learns to relate to other dogs and humans, so it is a good socializing exercise.

Before enrolling for such classes, it is important that you should go as a spectator. Some classes are rather harsh in their methods and, for a breed that becomes cowed if looked at 'loudly', these are not suitable. Ideally, these classes should exude an air of quiet discipline. I am always very wary of those where the humans shout and the dogs bark.

Basic Exercises

Until your puppy is old enough to go to organized classes you can start a daily programme at home. It is even better if you can get together with a few friends and their dogs. I begin very early, whilst grooming. The average puppy thinks this is a wonderful game and attempts to 'kill' the brush! I make it quite clear that he is to be still, and repeat 'Stand' as I groom him. As soon as he stops attacking the brush I praise him. Two or three minutes of such training each day is sufficient.

Training to walk on a collar and lead without lagging or pulling is the next essential. Some Golden Retrievers take to this very readily. Others need all your patience. The puppy's most usual response to the lead is to dash ahead, suddenly realize he is being restrained, whereon he proceeds to scream and throw himself about. Hold him firmly and gently, stroking and reassuring him in soothing tones. Alter your voice dramatically and deliver a sharp 'No!' the moment he starts to lunge about. Again, it is important for this lesson to last only a few minutes.

For the puppies who are determined to garotte themselves, whilst screaming hysterically, it often works to carry out such exercises in the company of an older dog with whom the puppy is familiar; his mother is ideal. Frequently, he will be so intent on mouthing her that the restraint offered by the collar and lead will become relatively unimportant. All of a sudden the puppy will be walking as if he had been doing it all his life.

Teaching the puppy to sit is another exercise which may be done at home before commencing any formal lessons. To teach this exercise, place one hand on the quarters and the other under the chin. As you push the chin up, press gently on the quarters saying 'Sit'. Ensure that this and all the other exercises are done in a relaxed and calm atmosphere to avoid any undue frightening of the puppy, which will hinder progress.

The next exercise is to teach your puppy to stay. This is done when he has mastered the 'sit'. Have him sitting at heel on your left. Put your hand in front of his nose in a blocking gesture and say 'Stay'. Move just one pace away from the puppy. If he obliges, return to him, then praise him enthusiastically. If he gets up, repeat from the first stage again. At this point keep hold of the lead all the time and, when he permits you to move one pace away, increase it to two, three, then four paces.

The next step is to have him sitting facing you. Stand close up so that he is looking up at you with his chin resting on your knee. Say 'Stay', and move back a step. If he remains in the sitting position, return and praise him. If he gets up, start from the beginning. Remember at all times that if your puppy disobeys, the reason is likely to be that you are not making yourself clear.

With the 'Stay', increase the distance and length of time for which he must stay until he will do a two-minute 'sit' and you are a full lead's length from him. When he is rock steady, drop the lead (do not remove it at this stage), and increase the distance. When you can be confident he will sit while you walk away to a distance the width of a church hall, you may take off the lead. Always make sure he understands when the exercise is over by the profusion of your praise.

Teaching the 'down', is more difficult than the 'sit' but, even so, should be quite quickly accomplished. There are two methods of starting this exercise: some people press in the centre of the back at the same time as they command 'Down'. I have found Golden Retrievers invariably become alarmed and resist. Another method is to place the dog gently in a 'down' position from the 'sit' by easing his front legs forward. At the same time, firmly pull the lead in the direction of the floor. Purists argue that this teaches a dog to break the 'sit' and go down. This is possibly so but, for basic obedience, it suffices.

At this stage of development, your puppy will be ready to go to formal obedience lessons to practise what you have taught him. At the same time, try to join up with up to six like-minded people who are wanting to train their Golden Retrievers at home.

Training to the Gun

The array of equipment offered by specialist firms is confusing. At this stage, all you will need is a rope lead with a ring at one end, which acts as both collar and lead. You will also need a whistle; the type made of horn is excellent. Fasten this round your neck with cord. A couple of dummies are essential. For the uninitiated, these are the cylindrical, green canvas shapes used for retrieving. There are those of medium weight and also the very heavy ones to simulate the weight of a hare or cock pheasant. I have found most puppies will happily take to a home-made sock-dummy rather than a new canvas one which smells strongly. In fact, there is no need ever to use a canvas one if your puppy prefers not to.

It is possible to purchase bright orange dummies which float. These are essential if you are intending to teach your puppy to retrieve from water. If you throw your green canvas one, or even your home-made one, into a lake, that is the last time you will see it, as it will sink instantly.

The first lesson in retrieving may commence at a very early age.

Bryanstown Cora retrieving a dummy over sheep netting.

Most Golden Retrievers will carry anything from the time they start to take an interest in their surroundings. One of mine will bring a single blade of grass if she is unable to find anything else. A small, soft woolly-sock, stuffed with another sock, is the perfect article for teaching the retrieve. Give your dog the command 'Sit' and place your arm around him to restrain him. Throw the sock and give the command 'Fetch', releasing him as soon as the sock lands. Most dogs will immediately pick it up and rush back, tail wagging. Do not grab the article from him but allow him to hold it for a minute. Be lavish with your praise. When you remove it, do so gently.

Next you can start with simple exercises to encourage your puppy to respond to the whistle. When you tell him to sit, give one short sharp blast on the whistle. Very soon you will be able to leave out the spoken command as he learns to react to the whistle alone.

Call your puppy to you, saying 'Come', then blow several short blasts. Soon he will associate these blasts with returning to you and the spoken command may be discontinued.

I cannot stress strongly enough the importance of having a dog who will respond to a whistle. Nor can I express the pleasure derived from owning such a dog. Bawling 'Come!' against a strong wind is totally ineffective and likely to result in a sore throat. The notes of a whistle carry quite clearly over considerable distances, even on windy days. Dogs tend to react far more quickly to the whistle than they ever do to the spoken command. It is also considerably more dignified to use a whistle than it is to shout at the top of your voice.

Continue to practise the 'sit' exercise, giving emphasis to the hand-signal. That is, raise the hand, palm facing the puppy, as you command 'Sit!'. Very quickly, the puppy will respond when you say his name followed by the hand-signal. Soon you will find the puppy watches you intently for the hand-signal.

Once he will sit reliably to a hand-signal you can start to train him to stop and sit by hand-signal, plus a blast on the whistle, when he is some distance away. Teach this exercise with patience, as a gundog who will stop on command is invaluable. Remember at all stages of your training programme that whilst training a dog is a relatively simple thing, untraining him is extremely complex. Dogs do not, in general, disobey because they derive pleasure from doing so. They disobey because they do not understand and are confused. If the dog becomes confused, you will need an enormous quantity of patience and perseverance to help him regain his confidence and understand what you require.

The single retrieve with a woolly sock can now be extended. Throw it into long grass, insisting he sits and waits a few moments before you command 'Fetch'. You are now training him to hunt by using his nose instead of his eyes, which is essential for a Retriever. Throw the article for short distances to begin with and, when you are confident he is truly searching, you may throw it over a much wider area.

Professional trainers use the command 'Get Out' when they send a dog for the retrieve article. I have always used 'Fetch' and find it adequate. The choice is up to you, but once you have decided which command to use, stick to it. It is the same with using the whistle: make sure you always use the same number of blasts for individual exercises. The dog does not reason in human terms, so your intention must be made quite clear.

Most puppies will progress quite naturally from a sock to a small dummy. If he refuses to pick up anything but the sock, do not be unduly concerned. Trainers' pre-occupation with dummies has always puzzled me. After all, no sportsman ever went dummy-shooting and required a dog to retrieve them. In spite of all the books which insist that the initial retrieving of canvas dummies is a pre-requisite for the eventual fully fledged Retriever, I have known good workers who went from socks to cold game and some who started on game, never having previously retrieved a sock or dummy.

For the purpose of these exercises, we will presume the puppy accepts the natural transition from wool to canvas. This is the moment when some simple directional training is needed. Practise throwing the dummy to one side of the puppy, then wave your arm in a most exaggerated way in that direction, commanding 'Fetch'. When he has retrieved the article, throw it to the other side, again waving in that direction. Regular practice will result in your dog paying great attention to the way you use your arms.

When the dog presents any article he has retrieved to you, it is important that you do not grab it immediately. Slip your hand gently under his chin, praising him all the time. The benefit of this is twofold: you are preventing him from prematurely spitting out the article, and you are teaching him that you will take it when *you* are ready.

Some dogs are keen enough to fetch the dummy but, having done so, make off as fast as possible in the opposite direction. I know of little that is more annoying, but it is imperative that your irritation is not detected by the dog. I even had one bitch who insisted on taking her dummy back to the car. It did not matter how far away the car was, she would run to it and sit by the tailgate and 'present' the dummy. I thought I would cure her by parking elsewhere and travelling the final half mile either on foot or in another car. She was far too smart for such deception and would take the dummy to any car she could find.

Resist your natural urge to chase the dog and dummy: you will never catch him and you will reinforce in his mind that running off is great fun. Run as fast as you can in the *opposite* direction, giving the whistled signal for the recall. It usually works. If not, you can resort to a fine check cord to persuade him to return. Instead of scolding, praise him vigorously, for it is the act of returning that you are rewarding.

My bitch, who insisted on running away with the dummy and presenting it to a car, was cured by having a series of retrieves in a narrow space between two barns. There was nowhere for her to go as the far end was blocked, leaving the only escape route behind me. She soon learned that it was great fun to bring the dummy to me and that she received much praise for doing so.

Your puppy needs to observe where the retrieve article falls and it is useful to enlist the help of a colleague for these lessons. Have your Golden Retriever sitting at heel and command 'Stay!' Give him a few seconds after the dummy has landed, so that you are in full control, then send him to retrieve it. Most Golden Retrievers love this exercise and, as his skill at marking and retrieving increases, you can vary the distances.

These first retrieves are practised out in the open but it is very useful to vary the dummy's landing point. Golden Retrievers love rushing into long grass and dense cover.

When your dog has progressed through these lessons and reached a reasonably competent standard, he may be introduced to the sound of gunfire. Most people are far too eager to get to this stage and, while I would agree that it is a most rewarding feeling to realize that your dog is steady to shot, do not be in too much of a hurry to get there.

I introduce my dogs to the sound of the gun with the aid of a starting pistol. It in no way resembles the sound of a twelve-bore shot-gun but it does make a loud bang. Be extremely vigilant regarding the distance between your dog and the gun. Many promising dogs have been ruined by being exposed to gun-fire at close range. One of my early bitches, Rossbourne Angelene, was perfectly steady until an over-eager person shot over her back. She squealed and bolted and was gun-shy for the rest of her life. She suffered enormously when my neighbour organized clay-pigeon shoots and it was some relief to us all when she became deaf.

To give a rough idea, the length of a football pitch would be a good distance from which to discharge a gun. Your dog, at the other end, will be aware of the bang but not subjected to it at close range. At this distance, most react with interest. Every time the gun fires, praise your dog and give an impression that this is all about enjoyment.

If you have commenced with a starting pistol at this distance, move gradually closer until the dog will accept the noise at a relatively close range. If your dog shows no obvious sign of concern, a shot-gun can be used, starting, as before, a full pitch's distance away.

Some dogs do exhibit considerable excitement when subjected to gunfire but this should be quite distinct from terror. Much has been written about gun-shy dogs and a certain mystique surrounds them. I have, in almost thirty years, owned two very gun-shy dogs. They were hysterically frightened and this would manifest itself in their shrieking and bolting. One would even froth at the mouth. The second one had never had an unpleasant experience with a gun and her brother was rock steady. In fact, he was almost oblivious and I believe that one could have shot over him with confidence. Nothing would persuade my bitches to accept the noise; they were demented with fright. Perhaps experienced trainers know of a method of curing gun-shyness. In my experience, a Golden Retriever who is shy remains shy.

Once your Golden Retriever is reasonably happy with the gun, you can employ the help of a dummy-launcher to project dummies a considerable distance. This is a hand-held appliance which will launch dummies, emitting a loud bang as it does so. The pitch is different from that of a gun and I have known dogs to be a little disturbed by the launcher yet be perfectly happy with the sound of a gun. But in general, if a dog is steady to one, he is steady to both.

The great advantage of a dummy-launcher is that it will send the dummy over a far greater distance than a human arm could throw it. Of course, this is only an advantage if your dog is a reliable retriever. Otherwise it means that you have a great deal further to go in order to collect your dummy!

Many people train with the launcher first, then progress to the gun. I have found it quite acceptable to train the other way round.

More directional training will be the next step. Although you have already covered the lessons of placing a dummy at each side of the dog and waving an arm in the required direction, there is a lot to be gained from several practice sessions to refresh your dog's memory. If he is obviously responding to your signals, you can become more adventurous.

Give your dog the command 'Sit' and throw two dummies, one to each side. Send him for the second one first. Most dogs will quite naturally go for the last to fall. At this stage, you are throwing the dummies by hand as you do not want them to travel too great a distance. After several retrieves of the second dummy, send your dog for the first. Invariably, he will go for the second. This is where the lesson of stopping on the whistle should be invaluable. The second he rushes for the wrong one, stop him on the whistle, redirect him to the first dummy and command 'Fetch'. If he does, praise him. If he does not understand, walk him up at heel so that he is much nearer the first dummy and tell him to fetch it. Most dogs have no trouble once they are taken nearer to the dummy.

When you think he understands what is required of him, repeat the exercise to reinforce what he has learned. Soon he will be retrieving two dummies in the order you choose, with no trouble at all. When he is reliable at responding to direction control, increase the number of dummies by one until you have five spread out and the dog will bring them in the required order. When you have reached this stage, you can feel reasonably confident that your dog is really working.

Try to end each lesson with one exercise that the dog really enjoys. It might be a straightforward simple retrieve or a chance to hunt for a dummy in thick cover. The favourite exercise will vary with each dog but I believe it is vitally important to end on an enjoyable note, for both the dog and the handler.

At this point, I add wings to the dummies. These are pheasant wings which have been exposed to the elements to dry them and remove any unpleasant odours. Hanging them up in an airy garage, or pegging them on the line in dry weather, usually makes them pleasant to handle. Tie them firmly around the dummy. The dog will normally show great interest in this new dummy and will happily retrieve it. Occasionally a dog will regard it with suspicion and refuse to pick it up. I covered a dummy with a piece of sheepskin for one dog who refused to retrieve the winged one and he picked that up quite happily, later progressing to the one he had first refused.

A little water-training adds interest to the lessons at this stage. Most Golden Retrievers will enter water with obvious enjoyment. In fact, the greatest problem with this breed is keeping them out of water, as anyone with an ornamental pond will know to their cost.

If your dog is reluctant to enter water, find a stream where the bottom is clearly visible and walk in yourself. At no stage force him, but the majority of Golden Retrievers would do anything rather than be left behind. Much praise will usually overcome any reticence. Taking another dog with you – one who loves the water – will nearly always overcome the problem. I find it makes a young dog a lot keener at the start if you make him sit at your heel and watch another handler working his dog in water. They usually react like small children and are desperate to 'have a go'.

I have not yet mentioned one of the most awful sins your dog can commit when working: making a noise (giving tongue). Any whining or yapping must be stopped as soon as it starts because, if you wish to enter any competitive form of gundog work, this is a disqualifying factor. Nothing is more humiliating than to be asked to leave a line because your dog has transgressed in this manner.

Once your dog is entering water on command and obviously enjoying it, you can start on the retrieving exercises. Remember to use the orange waterproof dummy at this stage. First let him see you throw the dummy across a very narrow stream and then send him for it. The idea is to increase gradually the distance of the throw and the width of the stream. Progress from one to two dummies and use the direction control learned earlier to make him retrieve them in the order you dictate.

When he is retrieving 'seen' retrieves from the opposite bank, the next step is to hide a dummy on the far bank and send him for it. Then hide two, and, as in the direction control lessons, make him retrieve them in order. The finding of these dummies is relatively simple but what is difficult is getting the dog to go out across the water for something which, to him, does not exist. It needs a great deal of control and frequent reversion to the 'seen' dummies on the far bank before some dogs will reliably perform this exercise.

Most Golden Retrievers are natural jumpers but there are those who definitely have to be taught to jump. I have seen kennels of dogs kept quite safely behind low sheep-netting. I have also seen ten-year-old Casamayor jump a 5-foot (1.5m) gate with monotonous regularity! Having jumped out, he will immediately jump back in, grinning all over his face. He definitely falls into the category of

Most Golden Retrievers are natural jumpers. Standerwick Franklin clearing a fence at an invitation working test, Gatcombe Park 1988. (Photo Cox)

'natural' jumpers! His sister Delmoss never exhibited his penchant for jumping and, when they were about a year old, Casamayor would dig furiously under fences. Delmoss would then squeeze through and he would jump over the top. It is as I said: there are those who do and those who do not!

I delay any sort of jumping exercises until my dogs are over a year old and then I must confess I do the minimum, as I am always so scared they will sustain injuries. Most of my training is confined to dry-stone-wall jumping. I find patting the wall is all that is needed to make most dogs jump over. If your dog is reluctant, taking an accomplished jumper with you is a great help. Rather like training to enter water, once they see another doing it they cannot wait to join in.

It is now time to introduce your dog to dead game. A pheasant must be in reasonable condition and not beginning to putrefy, as this will put off any dog and it will be very hard to convince him that all birds do not smell as bad. I have always obtained mine from the butcher. For a first retrieve, choose a hen pheasant. Avoid pigeons as their breast feathers tend to get stuck to the dog's mouth. If you have no alternative to pigeon, fit part of a nylon stocking, or a pop sock, over the whole bird and tie a knot in it so that it fits the bird tightly.

For the first lesson, tell the dog to sit and throw the bird a short distance. Then command 'Fetch'. Most dogs will retrieve perfectly to hand but there are those who refuse to pick up. I have one such dog and not only did he refuse, he expressed his displeasure by lifting his leg over the bird!

One who is reluctant to retrieve a pheasant will usually respond if you place the bird in his mouth, positioning one hand under his chin and commanding 'Hold'. Much patience is needed as it is exasperating to have a dog who refuses to pick up but if you let your annoyance show, it will take many lessons before you regain your dog's confidence.

Bryanstown Diplomat of Ulvin confidently retrieving pigeon at 7 months old.

When the dog is willing to hold the bird in his mouth with no obvious signs of resistance, walk backwards encouraging him to follow you, with your hand ready, under his chin, in case he should attempt to spit out the bird. Most Golden Retrievers soon progress to fetching a thrown bird.

Once the dog is reliably retrieving a small bird, you can progress to a cock pheasant, rabbit or hare. Remember that the weight difference between a hen and a cock pheasant is considerable and so is the size. It is important that the dog holds the bird correctly or it will trail on the ground and he will repeatedly tread on it. Any attempt to hold it by the head or wing should be positively discouraged. Dogs are very fond of carrying duck by their heads. Of course, this renders them very difficult to carry as they are badly balanced with all the weight near the ground. A smart dog will arrange the bird before picking it up and it is not unusual to see a Golden Retriever fold the head and neck over the body, so reducing the length before holding it.

The next thing to do is to arrange for a gun to fire as the pheasant is thrown, so simulating a shoot as near as possible. If you cannot attend a real shoot before attempting to qualify your show dog, do not worry unduly. I have gone straight from training to the qualifier, never having taken the dog on a proper shoot.

The Show Gundog Working Certificate

A dog may not enter for a Qualifying Certificate unless he has won a first prize at a Championship Show. No dog may run more than three times in total, in an attempt to obtain such a certificate.

If you have followed the steps of the training programme, the day itself should present little problem (apart from being rather nerve-wracking!) Arrive in good time to allow your dog to relieve himself. Remember to take with you a drink for yourself and your dog and some lunch. A change of clothing is essential because, if you are out all day in bad weather, you will be very wet indeed by the end of the day. Take a towel to dry your dog, and a meal to be given when he has finished working.

The accepted, almost uniform, dress for handlers on these occasions is a waxed jacket and hat, wellingtons, a warm sweater and trousers. Gloves are a good addition as you will find you do a lot of standing around and it can be very cold indeed.

The requirements of the Qualifying Certificate are that the dog is

Pheasant shoot, Balinacor, Ireland 1969. Michael Twist with Ir. Ch. Bryanstown Shannon of Yeo and Ch. and Ir. Ch. Bryanstown Gale Warning. These dogs gained 24 field-trial awards, including a first each in Open Stakes. (Photo Plunkett)

tested in line and must prove he is not gun-shy by being off the lead during gun fire. He must also prove that he is able to hunt and retrieve tenderly.

To give a clearer idea of what this is like in practice I will recount the events of the day when I ran Silk for her Show Gundog Working Certificate. I hope this account will persuade those who would like to have a go that there is nothing to be afraid of and everything to be gained.

It was the first time I had run a dog for the Qualifying Certificate, and it had never occurred to me before that the shoot is held for the benefit of the participants and is not organized for those trying to work their dogs. It is only the extreme kindness of the host who permits them to run.

We assembled in the farmyard half an hour before the start of the shoot and the judges explained the procedure for the rest of the day. We then walked to a field where the Guns were positioned ready for the day's sport. We were told to go forward and position ourselves, dog and handler being flanked on each side by a gun. We were told to remove leads and for a while nothing seemed to happen. A noise could be heard some way off, which I later discovered to be the beaters, who persuade the birds to desert the safety of cover and fly towards the guns. One moment all was still and I must admit to feeling extremely apprehensive and very cold. Silk repeatedly glanced up at me and written all over her face was the question, 'When am I going to do something?' No amount of training could have prepared me for what happened next. Suddenly the air was full of pheasant. I had erroneously imagined that the guns would fire in sequence but, of course, they all fired at once and birds dropped like hailstones. Many of the birds fell very close and I stupidly thought each dog would be asked to retrieve the closest bird. Wrong again! I should mention that out of our entry of over thirty, I was drawn to run third. The first dog was sent for a 'seen' retrieve and completed the exercise perfectly. The second misunderstood and shot through a gap in the hedge into an adjoining field. The handler eventually

Abnalls Evita of Standerwick tenderly delivering a live hen pheasant to Daphne Philpott at the Retriever Championships, Sandringham, 1987, where she gained a Diploma of Merit. (Photo Cox)

followed and, after what seemed a very long time, both returned and the dog performed a 'seen' retrieve.

The judge then asked me to send my bitch for a specific bird which was quite a long way away and definitely out of sight for the dog. My main worry was that she would have to pass many other birds on the ground on her way to retrieve the designated pheasant. She would also have to pass a neatly shot off wing and I wondered if she would bring this instead. I hardly dared breathe. I gave her the command and off she went, straight towards the distant bird, picked it up and returned, ears horizontal in the, 'Aren't I clever?', pose. It was only then that I began to feel a little more relaxed. I can truthfully say I have never had a day that was so nerve-wracking, yet so rewarding.

Next, we walked on to a field of shoulder-high kale. I will never forget how I felt at that moment. The densest cover we had trained in had been nothing like the height of this. Not only was the kale very tall, it was also planted very close. The judge explained that there was a pheasant at the base of a marker, which seemed to be so far away. I was requested to send my bitch in and at a wave from a steward hidden in the kale I was to call her out. What seemed like the impossible proved to be quite possible. I will long remember my relief when Silk's face, smiling from ear to ear, broke through the greenery and she completed a perfect retrieve.

I have included this description of my day to dispel some of the myths which surround the gaining of this award. I would like to dispel a few more. Before going, I was told by many people that the judges would be extremely unsympathetic to show dogs. Far from it. We were given every possible help and consideration. Every move was explained carefully and courteously and anything that was not immediately understood by the handlers was explained again. When a couple of dogs found the tests difficult, the judges were most understanding. At no time did I feel awkward or foolish. I was just so grateful to have expert guidance and determined that I would try to qualify all my dogs in future.

To those who are still unsure, I should like to add this as a further measure of persuasion. In the May preceding the qualifying date, my bitch had never had a single obedience lesson. She did not know what 'Sit' or 'Stay' meant and she certainly did not walk to heel. Before the day, she had only been exposed to one gun, never a whole line. We had never been on a shoot. I was a complete beginner too, yet Silk and I managed to learn the required skills in the intervening seven months. If we could do it, it is within the capabilities of anyone.

7

Showing and Judging

Once you have made the decision to show your dog, you will need to find out when and where shows are held. Two weekly publications, *Dog World* and *Our Dogs* carry advertisements for forthcoming shows and give the name, telephone number and address of the secretary, to whom you apply for a schedule and entry form.

All dog shows are held under licence from the Kennel Club. Shows are of various types and, whilst their titles are rather confusing, their actual function may easily be explained.

Primary Shows

Entry is restricted to members of the club holding the show and classes are for puppies and novice dogs. This means that only young stock, or older dogs who have won very little, may enter. This is a good place to start with your puppy but comparatively few of these shows are held each year. One judge will assess the whole entry.

Limited and Sanction Shows

Entry is confined to members of that society. Classes are often for varieties, i.e. mixed gundogs, rather than specifically for Golden Retrievers, Pointers and other breeds in the group. Champions may not enter these shows. One judge will do several breeds or, sometimes, at Sanction shows, will judge all classes.

Open Shows

Societies catering for all breeds or those interested in a single breed may hold such shows. At an Open Show held for most breeds, individual breeds will have separate judges. At a single-breed Open Show, one judge will officiate. Champions may enter for these but Challenge Certificates (the awards which contribute towards the title of Champion) are not on offer. Obedience classes are sometimes included.

Championship Shows

These are open to all breeds or are breed-specific. At a Golden Retriever Championship Show, there will be two judges, one for each sex, and also a referee, in case the judges cannot agree about Best of Breed. Sometimes there will also be obedience classes scheduled with a third judge. There are around twenty classes at a Breed Club Championship Show, starting with Minor Puppy (for dogs from six to nine months old). These classes may include Puppy, Junior, Special Yearling, Maiden, Novice, Undergraduate, Graduate, Post-Graduate, Minor-Limit, Mid-Limit, Limit, Open, Veteran and Field Trial. A list of definitions of each class is to be found in the schedule.

Matches

These are held by dog clubs, as a sort of practice show. They do not have individual classes but two dogs are assessed in each round, with the surviving two challenging each other at the end, the victor being declared Best in Match. Some societies challenge other clubs to matches and it is all good fun. It is also a splendid training ground for young stock, as the atmosphere of a real show is simulated. If you do not know of a dog club in your area, a letter to the Kennel Club, enclosing a stamped addressed envelope, will provide you with a list of those within travelling distance.

Exemption Shows

The Kennel Club needs to be approached for permission to hold such a show, which is exempt from its own rules. No more than four pedigree classes may be held and the other classes often provide much entertainment, being for 'The Dog Most Like Its Owner' or

'The Dog the Judge would Most Like to Take Home' or 'The Best Legs'. Events such as this are usually used to raise money for charity. They are also a good training ground for your puppy.

Cruft's

Despite the almost reverential way in which exhibitors speak the name, Cruft's is just another Championship Show. It is unique in the fact that one cannot automatically enter this show, as used to be the case. Now, it is necessary to qualify. Entries became larger and larger and some sort of selection to reduce the numbers was inevitable.

For many years, Cruft's was synonymous with Olympia and then Earls Court. Now it is held at the National Exhibition Centre in Birmingham.

Dogs who fulfil one of the following conditions may enter Cruft's:

1.   A dog under nine calendar months of age on 31 December is not eligible for entry at this show unless he has qualified for entry in the Kennel Club Stud Book. (N.B. A puppy so qualified which is between six and nine months of age is not eligible for entry in Special Puppy, Special Junior or Special Yearling.)
2.   A dog who, in the twelve months preceding Cruft's, has won a first or second prize in Minor Puppy, Puppy, Junior, Post-Graduate classes, or first, second or third prize in Limit or Open classes, at a Championship Show where Challenge Certificates were offered.
3.   Any dog who won a first prize at Cruft's the year before.
4.   A dog who has won his way into the Kennel Club Stud Book before the Cruft's entries close.
5.   A dog who has won a Green Star worth five points in Ireland under Irish Kennel Club rules.
6.   All champions, show champions, field-trial, working-trial or obedience champions.

To the novice owner, a dog who has won a first or more at Cruft's is held in awe, but to most serious breeders, a win at Cruft's would be placed second in importance to an equal award at one of the really prestigious Speciality Shows such as that held by the Golden Retriever Club.

Entering a Show

Read through your schedule carefully and study the definitions of each class. Pay particular attention to the age classes such as Minor Puppy, Puppy, Junior and Yearling. The age refers to the exact age of your puppy on the first day of the show (some shows are two-, three- or four-day events). It is so easy to make a mistake and many exhibitors, even the more experienced, would admit to making a mistake at some time. It is easier to be accurate when showing one dog, but surprisingly easy to become confused when showing several. If you enter the Junior class (for six to eighteen months), and then find on the day of the show that your dog is eighteen months old and one day, you will automatically be transferred to the Open class. This gives your eighteen-month-old Golden Retriever little chance of competing favourably against very mature dogs of, perhaps, five years old. Take care and remember it is your money you are spending.

Fill in your entry form in capital letters in ink. Some dogs have the most difficult names and the clarity afforded by capitals is essential. Check the date of birth and also the spelling of the sire's and dam's names. The printer will only copy what you write.

When deciding which classes to enter, do not be too ambitious. With an eight-month-old puppy, Minor Puppy is adequate. When he approaches nine months, most exhibitors like to enter Puppy as well. When your dog approaches twelve months of age it is prudent to enter Maiden and Novice. Check carefully the number of firsts you may win in Maiden and Novice, because if you unwittingly enter these classes when you have won out it is galling to find another exhibitor has reported you for contravention of regulations. The fact that you have entered in all innocence will not help you in the slightest and you will also feel very foolish at not having checked more thoroughly before entering.

Keep a photocopy of your entry form. I always write on the cover to remind me which dog I have entered, on which day it was posted and the number of the cheque which paid for it. As an added safeguard, it is wise to obtain a 'Proof of Posting' slip from the Post Office, which is free. If all this sounds fussy, permit me to recount the tale of the exhibitor who took his dog to an Irish Championship Show, only to find out, on arriving and reading his catalogue, that he had taken the wrong dog!

Also, if you arrive at the show and find your entries have not been received, it is very disappointing, especially if you have just driven two hundred miles or more. You may fill in another form and pay again but the Kennel Club will require proof that you originally entered by the closing date. They will not accept your word for it, neither will they accept a cheque book stub. The only thing that is acceptable is an official Post Office 'Proof of Posting' slip. Send your entry in good time, then prepare for the day.

Training for Show

Your show Golden Retriever will need to learn to stand while he is being examined and to move freely on a loose lead. He will also need to become accustomed to all the strange sights and noises he will encounter at shows.

The very best way you can prepare him for showing is to enrol at your local canine society and participate in their ringcraft classes. These sessions will enable you to practise standing your puppy while various 'judges' (usually members of the committee) handle him. Obviously, you can do a lot of the groundwork at home by handling him from birth and getting as many other people as possible to do this once he is vaccinated and the risk of infection has been removed.

Your puppy will need to stand still while his teeth are looked at. Do not choose to practise this when he is about twelve weeks old and his permanent teeth are appearing. His mouth will be very sore at this time and any unpleasantness associated with such an examination will remain with him for a long time.

He will need to become accustomed to hands feeling over his head, and to the judge standing in front and looking at him quite closely. Some breeds squirm visibly when stared at closely but Golden Retrievers are usually quite unaffected by close eye contact. It is useful to subject your puppy to ten minutes of this each day by getting members of the family to examine him.

Some puppies roll over and others sit as soon as you want them to stand still. I stand mine by gently lifting with one hand under the chin and one under the chest. When judging, I observe all sorts of undesirable methods of persuading a Golden Retriever to stand. The one that is most frequently adopted is putting an arm under his waist and hauling him to his feet. This not only alarms the puppy but the resulting roached (arched) outline is hardly the desired one.

Having lifted your puppy very gently into the desired stance, you will sometimes need to adjust the position of each individual leg. Just lifting and placing each foot in the required position is sufficient and a simple task to perform. Do this gently and positively, ensuring your puppy understands what is required of him.

To make the hindquarters of the dog stand four-square, various methods are adopted. I favour lifting the dog gently between the hind legs and then letting him down gently in the position you require. Even after this, it is sometimes necessary to place both feet separately in the exact position you require. A last-moment lifting and setting down of the hind leg nearest to the judge always results in an even better bend of stifle. You can feel the dog 'give' and so bend the joint further as you place him. Watch for the smart puppy who instantly moves his feet back into an undesirable position.

Do not annoy the dog with overlong exercises. Ten minutes a day is ample, coupled with one session at ringcraft class each week. The object is for him to stand looking happy and relaxed, with your hand under his chin. Ensure your fingers are neither clutching his jaw nor

The object is for your dog to stand looking happy and relaxed, demonstrated here by Linchael Cellini at Branjoy. (Photo Dalton)

Colbar Summer Mist showing to advantage with a little help from a pocket full of liver!

in any way visible from the judge's side, as this will detract from the picture. I remember having a photograph taken of my first champion on the day he won his first Challenge Certificate. I thought it was a wonderful picture and showed it to his breeder. My pride was a little flattened when she made the comment, 'Such a pity you were clutching his muzzle!'

There are some dogs who never will pose by being 'set up', with the handler holding chin and tail. However hard you try, the dog looks dejected and arches his back. If this happens, try free-standing your puppy. The easiest way to do this is to position yourself, with a pocket full of liver pieces, in front of your dog. Every time he assumes the correct stance, reward him with a piece of liver (grilled liver is less messy than the boiled variety). They learn very quickly that good behaviour results in lots of liver.

Your puppy will need to learn to move freely on a loose lead. He should walk briskly at your left side, neither lagging nor pulling. If he breaks into a run, he will be going too fast for the judge to assess his movement accurately. The judge will require you to move your puppy in a triangle and straight up and down. To the uninitiated this sounds like canine square dancing, but the moves are really quite simple. The handler moves his dog away from the judge to the right-hand corner, along the bottom of the ring to the left-hand corner, then back to the judge. The judge will then ask you to move away from him in a straight line to the bottom of the ring and back to him again.

The most experienced exhibitors, when asked to do a triangle, wander away and back again in the vague shape of an oval. A triangle means just that, so go right into the corners. I can imagine some of my showing colleagues smiling ruefully when reading this, as, when handling boisterous dogs, I have been known to move them in anything but a triangle! The move away from the judge and back to him is executed in a straight line. Make it as straight as possible. Fix a point at the end of the ring and move towards it, remembering to watch your dog, encouraging him as you move.

All this training can be done in your own garden but the most valuable way of doing it is in the company of other dogs and handlers. This will simulate the show scene as closely as possible. Hours spent practising at ringcraft classes pay enormous dividends later on.

Preparing for the Show

You will soon become accustomed to packing a show bag. A light-weight nylon bag is ideal as it has little or no weight. I find it convenient to pack a 'dog bag' and a 'human bag'. It makes finding things easier than if they are all packed together and, also, I would sooner carry two fairly heavy bags than one very heavy one. Some exhibitors prefer a rucksack, as this leaves their hands free. There are also bags with built-in canvas seats and although these are useful, I have never found the idea justified the extra weight.

In the dog bag, I pack a benching rug (a duvet for summer and a fur-fabric one for winter). I also pack two towels: one in case the dog gets wet and the other to pad the division which always seems to occur on my bench (and where tails or paws could be trapped in the gap). I also take dog food and water (if carrying water seems an unnecessary chore, remember that many dogs are upset by water from other areas and the last thing you want on the way home is a dog with diarrhoea). You will also need a water dish and feeding bowl. I take a brush and comb, thinning and straight-edged scissors. I find a small plastic spray-bottle is useful for spraying the coat with water if it has become ruffled during the journey. Your dog will also need a strong collar and chain to secure him on his bench. I like a collar which is part nylon webbing and part chain. This tightens if he pulls, preventing him from jerking his head out of it, which could have disastrous consequences, and loosens when he stops pulling.

The best sort of show lead is a fine nylon one with a ring at one end. Your clean show lead will stay clean in a plastic bag. It never ceases to amaze me how many spotlessly clean Golden Retrievers are shown on filthy leads. It is only seconds' work to scrub your lead and dry it.

In the 'human bag', pack a flask and food. An extra sweater is a must in our unpredictable climate. I always take a change of shoes as even the most comfortable old favourites seem to be made of cast iron by the end of a long day at a show. Apart from these essentials, keep a survival kit in the car. This might consist of a complete change of clothing in case you are too tired or too late to travel home that night. I also have a waterproof jacket and the uniform green wellingtons.

A word about what to wear when exhibiting follows naturally at this point. I know jeans are the universal uniform for all activities these days but I think they look scruffy and out of place in the show ring. Your attire should complement your dog. Ladies should bear in mind that their skirt forms a backcloth to their Golden Retriever. I remember seeing a beautiful Irish Setter shown by an exhibitor wearing an emerald green skirt. The whole effect was delightful. Golden Retrievers show up well against most colours, but avoid the obvious pitfalls such as a cream skirt or trousers which will exactly match your dog. It is advantageous to have at least one pocket into which you can put your liver and comb. Since exhibitors need to be able to move freely and quite fast, ladies should not wear stiletto heels and tight skirts. Avoid voluminous skirts which wrap around your exhibit's face when moving. Also, avoid loose floppy jackets which obscure your dog's head or topline as you bend over to 'top and tail' him.

If you are reading this wondering why it should matter what the exhibitor wears, I should like to draw your attention to some of the prestigious shows abroad where the exhibitors wear evening dress. The result is quite stunning. To dress all the exhibitors in jeans would detract considerably from this most delightful picture.

At the Show

Arrive at your show in good time. Remember there may be a long queue of cars waiting to get into the venue and if you are in the Puppy class it will be scheduled at the beginning of the day. Nothing will upset you and your dog more than arriving at the last minute for your début. You will be breathless, confused and irritable and, in that state, neither will do the other justice.

Exercise your dog when you arrive. If he relieves himself, it is your responsibility to clear up the mess. Make your way to your bench, or if it is an unbenched show, to the ringside. Chairs are provided at most shows but many exhibitors take the folding type with them. Collect a catalogue. Give your dog a drink, groom him and watch and listen for your class to be called. Check you are wearing your ring clip for your number, which must be worn in the ring. Remember, you may not wear anything which advertises your kennel affix.

Then relax. When you are called to the ring, listen to the steward and follow his instructions. He will ask you to stand at one side of the ring in a line. When you see the judge walking towards this line, all the dogs should be in that much-practised show stance.

The Judging

The selection of judges in Britain is a much more haphazard affair than elsewhere. Basically, all you have to do is wait to be asked. There is no formal qualification required and I must say that I cannot think of a suitable formal qualification which would suffice. The majority of judges are, or have been, exhibitors. Some have had years of experience of Golden Retrievers; others have never shown or even owned one. In fact, we have some judges who have never received a major award in the breed. This is regrettable but I hasten to add that such judges are in the minority. On the plus side, we have many people who are both knowledgeable and experienced.

To my mind, what makes a good judge is the ability to interpret the Standard and to place dogs in the order in which they most resemble it. The judge should totally disregard how the animals are bred and should show equal disregard for who owns them. If the handler of the best dog in the class has never ever awarded your dogs anything, this must not affect your decision. The excellent Golden Retriever represents excellence whatever the credentials of his owner.

I have heard judges criticized for putting up their own stud-dog's stock. But it is hardly surprising that they do this. After all, if a judge likes his own dog, and his progeny resemble him, it is wholly feasible that the judge will like them. Do not be too quick to criticize a judge's performance; wait until you are in his place and then see how easy the task is!

The judge must examine all the dogs thoroughly and then rank four or five, according to how closely they fit the Standard. When the entrants come into the ring, the judge will walk around the ring making an overall assessment of the quality of the class. Then the dogs will come forward to be examined individually.

The exhibitor moves to the appointed spot and either sets up (tops and tails), or free-stands his exhibit. The judge will step back to obtain an overall impression before examining your dog. The judge will run his hands over the dog's head and will often cup it in his hands to assess the proportions. He will observe the eye colour, check for a scissor bite and establish that all the premolars are present. He will feel the reach of neck and, most importantly, will feel from the point of the shoulder along to the angle of the upper arm and down to the forelegs. He will pass his hand between the forelegs to assess correct width. Some judges pick up the front feet at this stage. I have never seen any point in this. I like to stand back a little and assess the straightness of the forelegs and observe the feet, which should be tight and cat-like. By running his hands over your dog's ribs, the judge will be looking for a well-shaped rib-cage, neither too long nor too short.

The couplings (the space between the last rib and the hind leg) should be short. Your dog should be deep through the brisket. The judge will run his hand along the back and feel the tail set. If your puppy is male, the judge will check that he has two testicles descended into the scrotum. Any deviation from this is a serious fault. The bend of stifle will be felt and the muscling on the second thigh noticed. A final movement of the hand through your dog's coat away from the direction it grows, will ascertain the texture and condition of it, and whether he possesses the correct undercoat. This sounds a very complicated procedure but all takes place in about a minute.

You will then be asked to move your dog in a triangle, if the size and shape of the ring permits, and then straight up and down. If your dog leaps up or attempts to turn you into some sort of human maypole, do not be afraid to go back to the beginning and start again. I find a smile at the judge and a murmured 'Sorry' helps.

When all dogs have been examined, you will stand your dog in the show position again and the judge will walk around the ring once more before indicating the required four or five. Keep your eye on the judge to ascertain when his eye is on you. When I am judging, I like to have a look at five or six dogs, then turn back to look at those dogs as a group from behind. You would be amazed at what some of the exhibitors and exhibits are doing when I look back.

The judge will normally return to the centre of the ring for a final look and then will indicate which dogs he has selected. Make absolutely certain he has selected you before you walk to the centre. If you make a mistake it is quite humbling to have to return to your place! Some judges will call the dogs out in order. Others will say that they are not placing you yet, but would like certain dogs to remain. Listen carefully to what is said.

Try to be a good loser, even if you are crying inside. Congratulate the winners knowing that on another day you will all change places. These results are only the opinion of one person on one day. Next weekend it can, and often does, alter drastically.

Try to assess why these dogs won and yours did not. Be realistic;

Gaineda Chique-Chic is shown to advantage by being set up.

*Golden Retrievers are long lived. A young-looking Gaineda
Bucks Fizz aged 10 years, winning Veteran at Darlington
Championship Show 1990.*

kennel-blindness is a dreadful complaint. Remember, other people
do have good dogs and you must be able to see this if you are ever to
make an honest assessment of your stock.

Prizes

What you win very much depends on the type of show and the
society holding it. Many Limited and Sanction shows give rosettes
and cups. Some Open Shows give cash prizes and rosettes. Some
have a wonderful array of trophies but, in general, what you win is
the satisfaction of knowing you were first. The cash prizes hardly
ever cover your entries (or even the price of your catalogue!). If you
add the cost of your travel to and from the show to your entries, then
you are pounds out of pocket before you start.

The Championship Shows are, as their title suggests, where
champions may be made. In Britain, all the unbeaten first-prize
winners meet at the end of the dog judging and the best dog is

awarded the much coveted Challenge Certificate (referred to by exhibitors as a 'CC' or a 'ticket'). Dogs and bitches are judged separately. Three Challenge Certificates awarded to a Golden Retriever by three different judges entitle that dog to be awarded the title Show Champion. To become a full champion that dog must also gain a field-trial award or a Show Gundog Working Certificate.

If the aquisition of three CCs sounds easy, let me say that many exhibitors show for a lifetime without winning one. It is the quest which keeps us all going. Single Golden Retrievers have won over forty Challenge Certificates, some have won two and never managed to get the third.

The dog who wins the Challenge Certificate challenges the bitch CC winner and the better of the two, in the judge's opinion, is awarded Best of Breed. This dog then proceeds to the Gundog Group where he meets the other Best of Breed winners, such as spaniels, pointers and setters. A different judge will examine these and will pick a Group winner. This dog then challenges all the other Group winners and the chosen one is awarded Best in Show.

Showing and Judging Abroad

Very different rules govern the showing and judging abroad. I can speak with some experience on the Scandinavian system, although it differs slightly according to the country.

In each of these countries, the judge is required to make a detailed written critique of each dog. These are written as soon as each individual has been examined and moved. So you commit yourself before placing them in order at the end of the class. The judge is expected to include the faults as well as the virtues in these critiques, so they tend to be more soul-searching than the British ones.

All dogs entered in the class come into the ring. The judge has an initial glance and then they all leave the ring except for the first one to be examined. The judge will go over the dog, then move him, and then write the critique.

In most classes the exhibits are graded for quality. A first for quality means the dog is a very good representative of the breed and any very minor faults are categorized as 'unessential'. His merits will outweigh his faults. A second grading is given to dogs whose minor faults would still categorize them as good specimens of the breed, regarded as sound and typical. The third grade is given to a Golden

Retriever of good type whose faults would not be so pronounced as to deny that it was an 'adequate' representative of the breed.

If a dog is too playful to be assessed, no award is made and 'cannot be judged' is written on the critique.

A dog who exhibits any disqualifying fault under the Breed Standard in type or temperament is given an 'O'. The critique will show the reason for this award, e.g. 'O awarded as a result of an overshot bite'.

Having graded all the dogs in the Junior class, those awarded first are required to return to the ring. Those present are graded first to fourth. Any dogs considered to be outstanding examples of the breed are given an Honours Prize.

The Adult Class is graded as Junior but when those awarded first for quality return to the ring to be ranked first to fourth, the Juniors who were awarded the Prize of Honour accompany them. The winner of this class automatically receives the Challenge Certificate if the judge considers he is worthy of holding the title of Champion. No champions compete in this class.

The separate class for champions would, I am sure, be welcomed by many British exhibitors. How it would have changed our breed history when the dogs who were almost unbeatable were being shown. In this class, the judge writes a show critique and ranks the dogs first to fourth. Any dogs thought worthy of being Certificate quality receive a special award denoting this. The winner of this class does not receive a Challenge Certificate (which are awarded to non-champions only), but may compete for Best of Breed.

In Scandinavia, I have always found judging a most rewarding exercise. The shows are so well run and the hospitality of the organizers is excellent. Each judge has a secretary and a ring steward. The secretary writes, or types, the critique for the judge. The dogs are of a very high quality and most of the winners could compete favourably with the best in other countries.

In America, there is great support for the breed at shows. Dogs who become champions are referred to as Bench Champions and obtain their titles by collecting points according to the number of dogs they beat at each show. No more than 5 points may be won at a single show and to gain his title a dog must accumulate 15 points. As in Scandinavia, Champions have their own classes, so that promising and, possibly, younger dogs do not need to compete with them.

It is worth mentioning the Irish system of judging, as it also differs from the British method. Shows held in Eire are governed by the

Irish Kennel Club and no wins at British Kennel Club Shows may be counted towards Irish titles.

Irish entries are fewer for our breed than those at English shows. Green Stars are the awards equivalent to Challenge Certificates and these are worth from 1 to 4 points. Fifteen Green Stars are needed for a Golden Retriever to gain the title of Irish Champion, and this must include a 4-point Green Star or two 3-point Green Stars. If a judge who has previously awarded a dog a 3- or a 4-point Green Star gives such an award to the same dog again, this is only worth 1 point. To become an Irish Champion, a dog must also gain an award at a field trial or must attain a Working Certificate at a field trial. The dog is only eligible to enter for such a certificate after he has won a Green Star. The title of Show Champion is now recognised.

Writing a Critique

Judges in Britain are expected to write a critique on all the dogs placed first at Open Shows and those placed first and second at Championship Shows. Unlike Scandinavia, a detailed critique is not written in the ring and given to the owners, but brief notes are made instead. After the show, a detailed critique is written.

British judges often write at length about the virtues tending to take the view that omission suggests the faults. In Scandinavia, the judge is required to mention faults and virtues. Some British exhibitors become very upset if you refer to the shortcomings of their dogs in these reports, which are published in the two weekly dog papers. I believe faults can be mentioned in a tactful way and I think we do the breed in general a disservice if we do not do so.

Most judges work through the points of the dog from head to tail when writing a critique, so the piece could read as follows:

> 1. Lovely head and expression with dark eye. Good reach of neck. Shoulders well laid back with good angulation of upper arm. Straight front; good tight feet. Ribs well sprung and correct short couplings. Level topline. Very good bend of stifle and correct hocks. Good tail set. Moved well with strong driving action.

Sometimes it is not necessary to write so much about the second dog, especially if you thought he came second by a very narrow margin. It would suffice to write:

2. Another lovely dog who possessed many of the virtues of my winner. I felt his movement was a little less positive and, as yet, he lacks maturity.

This shows your reason for placing him second and the criticism is made in a diplomatic way. In a breed as numerically large as ours, it is important to state your reasons for placing the dogs in a specific order.

Be positive in what you write. Avoid meaningless comments like, 'very much my type'. The dog should be of a type which fits the Breed Standard rather than one that just happens to look like those in your kennel. Another pitfall to avoid is overdoing the word 'nice'. To write, 'Nice head and expression. Nice shoulder. Moved nicely' is open to personal interpretation and means very little.

Exhibitors pay very dearly to show their dogs and should at least be rewarded with your reasons for placing them as you did. If you cannot put these reasons into words, it suggests you are not sure of them. Most exhibitors, even experienced ones, scan the dog press for the reports of their wins. It is very disappointing when no mention is made of your triumph and rather suggests that the judge did not feel your dog was worth writing about.

When writing your critique it is a very good idea to have the Standard beside you, even if you think you are fully conversant with your subject. Remember, hundreds of people will read what you write, so make doubly sure you do not inadvertently make a mistake. It is very difficult to argue your way out of a mistake in print.

I recently read a report of a Golden Retriever that had been placed first at an Open Show and the judge said: 'Correct deep gold coat.' What a blunder! This suggests that the range from cream through to mid-gold is incorrect. Preferences must be kept to yourself. You are judging to a set of rules clearly stated by the Kennel Club and your own personal preference must not come into the interpretation.

A great deal can be learned about a judge's ability from the way he writes a critique. By that, I do not mean your remarks should resemble an extract from a degree-examination paper. Most of the words and phrases you require are present in the Breed Standard. All you have to do is, using the written word, compare the dog to this Standard. Say in which respects he fits and fails, but make your comments in a way that will not be seen as tactless.

Sometimes, what we actually mean is not instantly obvious by what we say. For instance, when I write, 'pleasing head', I *do* mean that the appearance of the head and expression pleased me, yet I can remember using the expression in a critique I wrote abroad and the owner said it was obvious that I had not liked her bitch's head or I would have written, 'Good head'. Another instance of misinterpretation occurred when I wrote, 'Too long for her height'. The exhibitor argued that this could only be correct if it was written, 'too short for her length.' I have never been able to see even a subtle difference between those two!

Judging for the First Time

When you arrive for your first appointment, calm yourself by considering that you are there because you were thought competent enough to officiate. The exhibitors obviously agree with the appointment or they would not have entered.

Arrive at the show in good time, so that you have time to go to the lavatory, and have a cup of tea. If you have driven a long way you will need time to wind down. If the distance is excessive, it is a very good idea to arrive the day before.

You will notice that fellow exhibitors undergo a strange transformation when you arrive. They dare not acknowledge you and you hardly know how to treat them. There is nowhere for you to go until you start judging. You cannot chat to the exhibitors as you would if you were showing your dogs. Many times I have watched breeds in which I am not even slightly interested, merely to fill the awkward gap between arriving and judging.

It is amazing how nerves disappear once you start to examine the dogs. I can only liken it to taking an examination. The tension, moments before the invigilator indicates that you may begin, is incredible, but as soon as you start writing, it evaporates. So it is with judging. The moment you have waited for and worked hard for has arrived and as soon as you place your hands on the first dog, there is a sense of familiarity mixed with relief.

Do not be overawed by the presence of one or more very experienced exhibitors. It is a compliment to you that they are there but the very fact that they are there means they have faith in your ability, so have faith in yourself. Remember that all these 'famous' people judged their first show once.

Afford the same courtesy to a six year old handling a Golden Retriever as you do to the person who owns several champions.

Win or lose, it is important that each exhibitor believes he has taken the best dog home. The rosette reads, 'Thrown out with the best'!

They have all paid their entry fees. I always preface any instructions with, 'Please' and, after these have been completed, respond with, 'Thank you'.

Female judges are well advised to check their appearance in the mirror before they leave home. A skirt which is a smart length when standing can become revealingly short when bending over a dog. The elegant slit at the back of your skirt will extend considerably higher when you reach over a Golden Retriever to feel his spring of rib! So check your rear view as you bend over an imaginary dog.

The men are not exempt from inadvertently giving rise to humour. I remember an elegantly dressed man, wearing a cream linen suit, who was totally oblivious to the fact that his Mickey Mouse boxer shorts showed quite clearly through his trousers. It livened up the day!

Every judge should be able to say quite honestly to himself that he truly placed the dogs in order of merit as he perceived them, irrespective of who owned them or how they were bred. If you do a

134

good, honest job, you will be rewarded with many more judging appointments. Your name will be included in the judging lists kept by breed clubs and you will be regarded as a person whose opinion is well worth having.

Do keep a detailed record of judging appointments. When you are asked to judge a Championship Show the Kennel Club requires you to fill in a questionnaire with details of all previous judging experience. You need to put the name of the society you judged for, how many classes and the number of dogs in each class. Most importantly, you need to state the date of each show. No one warned me about this and at the beginning the idea of judging a Championship Show seemed too improbable to consider. Consequently, I kept no records at all and when I was asked to fill in my questionnaire, I had to write to secretaries asking when I judged their shows. Knowledge of what might be required one day would have saved me a great deal of time and effort.

8

Breeding

The world is full of unwanted dogs. Some are the results of matings which were accidents but, sadly, a large number are pure-bred animals who were brought into existence by people for a variety of reasons. It saddens me even more to realize that the dogs' homes are largely populated by dogs who were wanted when they were appealing fluffy bundles. Unfortunately, this appeal diminished rapidly when they wet carpets and chewed chairs, often as the result of being left alone for hours while their owners were out at work.

Breeding dogs is a serious business. It is not for the faint-hearted; neither is it a way to get rich quick. There will often be more disappointments than successes and there will be times when so much goes wrong that you wonder why you bother.

The responsible breeder seeks to improve the breed, only breeding from animals who are true representatives of the breed in both conformation and character. He subjects his stock to regular heredity checks and would never breed from any animal that did not pass. He breeds from his bitch because he believes the animal is so good that it has much to give. He selects the very best stud-dog available, resisting the urge to use the 'convenient' one in the next village.

The responsible breeder rears puppies to the best of his ability; they lack for nothing. He vets prospective buyers and makes every possible move to ensure they are suitable owners for puppies.

This responsible breeder completes all the documentation to hand over at the time of purchase. He takes care to give as much help as possible and maintains contact with the new owners for the puppy's life. He also accepts responsibility for anything that goes wrong which may be attributed to him, and agrees to make restitution.

If breeding is such a serious affair and is so fraught with difficulties, why do we do it? It is the constant search for excellence which keeps me going; the quest for perfection, which always eludes me in its complete form, but allows me to get tantalizingly close.

Breeding dogs is a serious business.

Breeding livestock of any type is a humbling experience. Just as you are producing sound, healthy winners and complacency begins to creep in, that is the very time when disaster will strike. This is when one puppy, from clear parents, will prove to have cataract, or one from very low-scoring parents will have a very severe grade of hip dysplasia.

Such set-backs have a numbing effect initially and then one of two situations arises: you will either feel the odds are so stacked against you that you cannot continue; or you will be more determined than ever to succeed. It is for those who fall into the second category that this chapter has been written.

Selecting your Bitch

The bitch who is to be the foundation of your line must be as typical of the Breed Standard as possible. She should, ideally, come from several generations of Golden Retrievers with low hip-scores and clear eye certificates. She should also be of sound temperament.

A kennel's foundation bitch should be typical of the Breed Standard, as is Nor. Ch. Majic One Step Ahead.

It is not easy to come across such a bitch and most aspiring breeders start with a puppy bitch, having to wait until she is old enough to have her hips X-rayed and her eyes tested. Sometimes your promising puppy bitch, who has started her show career so well, will need to be discarded from your breeding programme at this stage, because one of the heredity checks has exposed a flaw. If you are keen enough to breed Golden Retrievers, this will upset you but will not make you lose sight of your goal.

The first five Golden Retrievers I had, all from reputable kennels, proved to have cataract. I found the news devastating, especially when one was diagnosed at eight years old. This dog had been used extensively as he was the end of a very famous line. He had also been tested by our most eminent eye specialist for each year of his life. Then another superb bitch was found to have it. I remember driving home from that examination session feeling as if the world had come to an end.

At that point, I was given a good talking-to by another eye specialist, whom I have grown to respect enormously and to whom I owe a great deal. He told me to stop wallowing in self-pity and to start again. He said if I was really keen to succeed, nothing would stop me. I was keen and his wise words struck just the right chord in my reasoning. If others could obtain and produce clear stock, then it had to be possible for me to do it. It was.

It is possible to obtain a sound, typical, young adult who is clear of hereditary defects. Sometimes such a bitch will become available when an exhibitor, who has been running on two, makes his choice and the other is surplus to his needs. Such bitches do not come cheaply and it is right that they should not. Much planning, time and money has been involved in the production of such an animal, and it never ceases to amaze me just how cheaply some would-be breeders expect to acquire one. I have received calls for puppies from people saying, 'I am wanting a bitch who will be a top winner, have a very low hip-score and will have clear eyes.' I reply, 'So am I!'

For an eighteen-month-old bitch who is a sound, typical specimen of the breed, it is reasonable to be asked to pay over four times the price of a puppy and, if she is a top winner as well, considerably more. If you want that particular bitch enough, any price that is asked for her will seem acceptable.

Breeding from your Bitch

Long before your bitch is in season you should have formulated your plans for having her mated. I like to mate my bitches at their third season but this is dependent on the intervals between seasons. Some go six months, while others have a year between seasons. If at the time she comes into season you have not decided which dog to use, it is wise to wait until the next time. Hurried decisions are not to be recommended.

If you are breeding for the first time, the selection of a stud-dog for your bitch will seem an impossible task. You will feel overawed by the large number of dogs available but once you work out the type of dog that will be most suitable for your bitch, the field will narrow considerably.

The chosen dog should complement your bitch, by which I mean that he should excel where she fails, or he should be even better where she is already very good. If she lacks length of neck, then, ideally, the stud-dog should have a good reachy neck and if his sire and dam possessed this virtue, so much the better.

It is not enough for the dog to be of a type you admire: he must suit

The chosen stud-dog should suit your bitch in looks and breeding. Sh.Ch. Camrose Tulfes Intirol. (Photo Dalton)

your bitch in both looks and breeding. We can all produce champions on paper and if it was so easy, all the champions mated to champions would only produce champions. I am relieved to say this is not so, because if such things were certain, all the striving for excellence would be possible in a single generation.

Two courses of action are open to you in your selection of the dog for your bitch. You can either line-breed or out-cross. If I mention line-breeding to novices they get very concerned about what the breeding of animals too closely related to each other might produce. This is in-breeding, which is quite different. In-breeding involves mating closely related animals together, such as mother to son, brother to sister, father to daughter. At one time, when the number of Golden Retrievers was few, this method was employed, with all its attendant difficulties, but it is seldom used today. Such matings produced some superb specimens of the breed in looks but they also doubled up on hereditary faults, often with disastrous consequences.

Line-Breeding

Line-breeding is close breeding employed in moderation, with a working knowledge of the animals involved. This is where the pedigrees are of great importance. The idea is to minimize the faults in the breed by mating animals who do not possess similar faults. For this knowledge, the novice has to rely on the honesty of those who either owned or bred those dogs, or, to a less reliable degree, to those who remember them. The more shown dogs there are in the pedigree, the easier it will be to trace what you are looking for.

Avoid the dog who possesses a pedigree which is largely composed of unknown dogs. Even if this dog is the most wonderful animal you can find, it is safer to go for one slightly less wonderful who carries a pedigree of known dogs. Unknown dogs in a pedigree may have retained their anonymity for a number of reasons, but there is always the possibility that they never reached the show ring because of an obvious fault. If you are unaware of the nature of this fault,

The result of line-breeding: Linchael Cellini at Branjoy, Linchael Chantilly and Sh.Ch. Linchael Cartier of Gloi at 7 months old. (Photo Lindsey)

you cannot avoid perpetuating it if your bitch is carrying the same one.

I am not disputing that somewhere, even as I write, there is the most perfect specimen of a Golden Retriever lying by its owner's fire. He has never been shown because his owner is too busy. He has a 0:0 hip score, clear eyes and a perfect temperament. But such dogs are indeed rare.

Do not go to extremes in your quest for excellence. If your bitch is good all round, except for a rather narrow head, do not choose a stud-dog with the coarsest head you can find. This will not balance your bitch's lack of head, and the most likely result is that some of the puppies will be as weak in head as their mother, whilst others will be as coarse as their sire.

Line-breeding is a certain way of establishing virtues in the line of your choice but remember, it cannot put there anything which is not already present in your dog and bitch and their ancestors. It will provide the undesirable as well as the desirable characteristics. By that, I mean if your bitch is slightly straight in stifle but has lovely dark eyes and you mate her to a dog who has the same lovely dark eyes and a reasonable stifle (but his sire and dam had mediocre stifles), you cannot choose to perpetuate the correct eye colour but discard the straight stifles. The genetic make-up is present for both characteristics and you will get both, in varying degrees, whether you want them or not. To have the characteristics we require while discarding those that are undesirable is to enter the realms of genetic-engineering, upon which subject one could moralize indefinitely.

Some breeders use line-breeding to correct or balance a fault but care must be taken that in the search for one goal the sight of the whole dog is not lost. Breeding is all about balance and sometimes it is tantamount to juggling. It is of little use producing the most beautiful Golden Retriever head imaginable if the rest of the dog leaves much to be desired. Better to have a slightly less spectacular head than to sacrifice the complete body. We can all give examples of breeding programmes where such dogs have been the result.

Line-breeding necessitates keeping in one's mind the virtues and shortcomings of as many animals in the proposed litter's pedigree as is possible. Mentally, you need to draw up 'for' and 'against' columns when planning such matings. To give a personal example, my dogs have had very good shoulders and upper arms for generations.

Therefore, when planning to line-breed to dog 'X', who lacked a little in this department but had everything else I wanted, I would risk it. If my bitch had forehand construction that was mediocre and came from generations of similar animals, it would be pointless to line-breed to dog 'X'. He might have everything else but his shoulders linked with those of my bitch would virtually guarantee mediocrity in this area for the progeny.

At the end of the day, it is all remarkably simple and one does not have to be a geneticist to predict the construction of the progeny that will result from some matings. Time after time, I hear experienced people discussing their disappointment that dog 'A' mated to bitch 'B' produced puppies who did not come up to their expectations. They are genuinely amazed that two such lovely animals could have produced such a fault. Yet, if they were to look dispassionately at the animals in question, they could see quite clearly that both exhibited this fault which made it a certainty in the progeny. Often they were so single-minded in their determination to establish several virtues that they simply did not see the pitfalls. This kennel-blindness can only hinder the improvement of the breed.

Sometimes breeders will use a line-bred dog on a line-bred bitch but on each side the line-breeding will be to different strains. The results from this can be spectacular because the progeny are so good – or so bad! Some very good results may be obtained in the first generations but continuity breeding poses a problem for future generations and it is a rather hit-and-miss affair.

If you feel you would rather not line-breed, the other course available is to out-cross. Everyone has to do this at some time and I am just at the stage where I have line-bred for so many years that I feel I will have to plan in this direction.

Out-Crossing

To out-cross means to mate unrelated animals or animals that have few common relatives. This method is often inadvertently employed by breeders who decide to use the top champion of the day on their bitches, irrespective of whether he suits them or not. When the progeny do not inherit their sire's excellence, some breeders will complain that the dog cannot be much good or he would have produced better puppies for them. The dog is not a magician and is not wholly responsible for the resulting litter.

Some breeders make the positive decision to out-cross and while the resulting litters might contain one or two quality animals, it is difficult to predict the outcome with any degree of accuracy, which one may when line-breeding.

The last, and only, time I out-crossed, I mated a show champion bitch, who included Best of Breed at Cruft's among her awards, to a dog of excellent construction who had produced Championship Show winners and whose added attraction for me was that he was a known hip-improver (i.e. one who stamped low hip-scores on his progeny). He possessed many qualities that I admired, including a wonderful outgoing, fearless temperament. He was equally at home in the middle of heavy gunfire as he was being patted by small children or playing games. I felt my bitch could do with more confidence and that she would benefit from his dense, double coat and lovely dark eye.

On paper, these animals had a couple of common ancestors way back, but most of the dogs featuring in the proposed litter's pedigree were unrelated. The result was total mediocrity. What I had failed to take into account was that the dog and bitch were of totally different

Alresford Nice Fella, a stud-dog owned by Eva Harkness.
(Photo Boreland Studio)

144

types. This taught me a great deal, mainly that the sire and dam must *look* right for each other and this, for me, must over-ride whatever the pedigree tells me.

How can you tell if the animals in question look right for each other? I like to imagine that I have a photographic negative of each and when one is superimposed upon the other, there is a positive likeness. It is a useful mental exercise to try.

Having chosen your dog, the accepted procedure is to approach the dog's owner. Bear in mind this should take the form of a request, not a statement. The owner has the right to accept or refuse bitches as he thinks fit.

When you ask to use a particular dog, be prepared to say how your bitch is bred, stating her sire and dam and also quote her hip-score and the date of her latest eye certificate (which should be right up to date). Above all, do not be embarrassed to ask the price of the stud fee. Over the years I have been amazed by the rumours surrounding certain dogs' fees. Most stud-dog owners advertise in the various

Sh.Ch. Concorde of Yeo, a well-used stud-dog.

handbooks that their dog will be at stud that year and state the current fee.

Tell the owner when you expect your bitch to be in season and ask him how he wishes you to proceed. Most stud-dog owners will ask you to contact them on day one of her season and if the dog you book is well used, it is imperative that you do this to prevent his being booked on the very day when your bitch is ready.

I am frequently asked what I consider a fair stud fee. I can only say that I believe stud fees are too low in Britain where they are not even the price of a puppy. Elsewhere, it is accepted practice to pay a fee on mating, then an agreed sum for each live puppy born. I can only reiterate what I said about a fair price for a bitch: if it is what you want, the price will be worth it.

Buying your own Stud-Dog

To own a stud-dog might have obvious appeal for the would-be breeder. After all, to have a dog on the premises would do away with the guesswork of when your bitch is ready. It would also render unnecessary the long journeys to reach the stud of your choice (who always seems to live at the very opposite end of the country from the bitch!)

However, there are drawbacks to having your own stud-dog. It is not a viable proposition to keep a stud-dog for only one or two bitches. The idea of keeping a dog is not just for your own bitch but so that other bitches may come to him. He will be competing with many well-used stud-dogs and some of them will be champions. Unless he is shown and is a top winner, his appeal will be limited and his services restricted to a few local bitches, or those belonging to friends.

Stud-dogs are not intended to be used irregularly. Ideally, a regular stream of bitches should be booked to him. Unless you are reasonably certain of this, it would be better to think again.

Once you have used your own dog and perhaps retained a bitch puppy from that mating, remember he cannot be used on that puppy when she reaches adulthood, as they are too closely related. The pick of the stud-dogs is at your disposal, so it is not necessary to burden yourself with one. However, you may wish to keep a stud-dog because you really like the males and enjoy stud-work.

In some breeds, the keeping of a stud-dog is a difficult business,

Two of the excellent stud-dogs of the present day, Sh.Ch. Melfricka Zed and Melfricka Ace in the Hole. (Photo Pearce)

but I have always found Golden Retrievers to be perfect gentlemen, exhibiting none of the unpleasant traits sometimes found in other breeds. I can truthfully say that I have never had a moment's unpleasantness between my dogs and they all live together. The only way they are affected when the bitches are in season is that some go off their food for a few days. I know of no way of preventing this. My way of coping is to ensure that they are carrying enough weight before the bitches are due.

If you decide to keep a dog, you will need to be able to separate him from the bitches when they are in season. Some people manage quite well in a house, but I think this is difficult. Doors can so easily be left open and Golden Retrievers are remarkably adept at opening even the most intricate fastenings. One of my dogs loves to amaze visitors by suddenly walking into a room on his hind legs, paws on the handle! We have turned the handles upside-down, but he worked that out in minutes, and since he is also skilled in the turning of door knobs, it would be very difficult to isolate him in a house of in-season bitches.

Some dogs will chew their way in or out of almost anywhere to get to bitches, and the bitches are not exempt from employing the same tactics to get in. I include this as a warning for those with beautiful, panelled wooden doors who have it in mind to leave their stud-dog on one side and their in-season bitch on the other.

Be prepared to have your formerly ordered life-style disrupted if you keep a stud-dog. The times when bitches arrive will seldom be the most convenient. By the law of averages, most come at meal-times and have been known to come before breakfast or when all the family had retired for the night. These times are seldom when they had arranged to come. Particularly exhausting are those who arrive really late the night before a Championship Show. You have trimmed and bathed your exhibits and all you can think of is a bath and bed, when the barking of the dogs alerts you to a car in the drive. The fact that you are setting off at 4 a.m. to drive over three hundred miles seems to have little meaning for your visiting bitch who flatly refuses to co-operate. If none of this puts you off keeping your own dog, the next section should help.

Training your Stud-Dog

In my experience, there are two main categories of Golden Retriever stud-dog: those who do and those who would prefer not to. The young dogs who know instinctively what to do and get on with it are a joy. The reluctant boys make life a little more difficult.

Ideally, start your dog with an older bitch who has been mated before and does not object. The flirtatious bitch will sometimes be so keen that she scares the novice stud-dog. It is better to opt for the bitch who gazes at the ceiling and 'thinks of England'. This type is usually unaggressive and makes handling your dog easy.

Before mating, examine the bitch's certificate of freedom from hereditary eye defects and check her hip-score sheet. At the same time, show the owner your stud-dog's certificates and score sheet.

Some stud-dog owners allow the dog and bitch to play together before attempting to mate them. This is a splendid idea, but only if you are certain the bitch will not snap and frighten your young dog. Such foreplay will usually make the slightly reticent bitch lose all her inhibitions.

If he sniffs her and attempts to mount, you are in business. Even if she is the sweetest, most co-operative bitch in the world, ensure that she is held by her collar. Ideally, the handler will stand facing her and will firmly grasp her collar with a hand at each side, over the top of her head, just behind her ears. If you are even slightly unsure of her reactions, she should be muzzled to prevent her snapping at the dog.

It is never easy to ascertain whether a bitch is quite ready for mating but the following is a reasonable guide. Insert a clean finger, well smeared with petroleum jelly, into the bitch's vulva. Make sure your nail is very short to avoid damage. With the tip of your finger you will feel a muscular ring. If your finger slips through this ring relatively easily, the bitch is ready. If the ring is too tight to admit your finger, she is most certainly not ready.

The person who holds the bitch has a very important job. So many people hold the bitch firmly until the moment the dog penetrates and then, as the bitch jumps, lets go. For this reason, owners are not always the most suitable people for the task. A kennel maid experienced in stud-work, or another stud-dog owner, would be ideal.

Delay the actual mounting of the bitch by your dog until you are in the right position. It is useful to have a piece of matting to kneel on and this will also prevent the dog's feet from slipping. I also have a small rubber bucket, which, when inverted, makes a comfortable seat for the duration of the mating.

Kneel down facing the bitch's tail and encourage the dog to mount. Place your hand under the bitch, between her hind legs so that the vulva is between two fingers. This is so that you can feel if the dog is in the correct place, because you will not be able to see what he is doing. Dogs who miss the vulva and aim too high or too low are a nuisance and soon get into this habit, which is difficult to break.

It helps to apply petroleum jelly to the vulva and, if you also smear some on the long hair of her trousers, it will keep it out of the way and make it much easier for the dog to penetrate. Some bitches have such profuse hair on their hind legs that it does impede the dog's action unless it is smoothed out of the way.

Some breeders attempt to insert the dog's penis into the vulva but I believe this makes the dog do one of two things: either he will become totally reliant on you, or he will become very touchy and jump away as soon as he thinks you are going to touch him. Remember, at all times, that you are dealing with a highly sensitive part of the dog's anatomy and the lightest touch from you will cause him to thrust and start to ejaculate. It is important that he should not do this until he is 'tied' to the bitch. This is when the bulbous gland at the base of the penis swells inside the bitch and holds the two animals together. Until this tie is effected, the dog can easily slip out of the bitch, especially if she pulls away.

This tie may last anything from ten to sixty minutes. Obviously the dog would be far too heavy for the bitch for such a length of time, so it is important to make them more comfortable. Some dogs will automatically drop themselves to one side of the bitch at the front end, while still tied. Others will dismount at the front, then raise one hind leg and turn so that both animals are facing in opposite directions, tail to tail. Whichever position you or your dog decide upon, ensure all manoeuvres are made calmly and smoothly to avoid frightening the participants. Hold them throughout the tie, as either dog pulling away is extremely uncomfortable for the partner. Also, any discomfort felt at this stage will be potentially off-putting for the future.

All the time the dog is tied to the bitch, she is receiving semen and, when the tie ends, there is some leakage, which often alarms onlookers. This is surplus to requirement and will not reduce the bitch's chances of becoming pregnant. Some stud-dog owners like to raise the bitch on her front legs as if she is doing a hand stand. I have never subscribed to this practice as I tend to avoid doing anything that may alarm the bitch.

Some owners do not like to be present at the actual mating. They elect to remain in the car or house. Sometimes they are quite simply embarrassed, sometimes, they do not want to see the bitch they love dearly being subjected to what they feel must be an unpleasant experience. They might have children with them and do not wish them to witness the act. Whatever the reasons for their absence, it is sound practice to invite them to witness the tie, even if for just a few seconds. Their presence at this moment is unlikely to upset the bitch, who will by that time be pre-occupied, and it will prevent any dispute if the bitch, for some other reason, does not conceive.

At the completion of the mating, offer the dog a drink of water, then ask the owners to return her to the car. You can then complete the paperwork. Ensure that each of you ends up with the correct set of documents.

As the stud-dog's owner, you should fill in the official Kennel Club form on which the bitch's owner will register the expected litter. On this, you write the dog's registered name and his number. You fill in your name and address and the date on which the mating took place. You sign this and hand it to the owner, who will eventually fill in his name and address and will list the chosen names for the puppies. The owner will send this off with the appropriate fee to the Kennel Club (*see also* the chapter on whelping, page 164).

It is at this point that the owner will usually pay the stud fee. It is surprising how many people forget this in the excitement of having successfully managed a mating. Most owners ask what will happen if their bitch fails to conceive. The accepted practice is to allow a free repeat service. It should be stressed that this is completely at the discretion of the dog's owner and is in no way obligatory. I have always offered a free repeat and would expect the same courtesy to be afforded to me by other breeders. I was a little annoyed to be charged for a repeat mating several years ago. The bitch missed that time as well, even after I had paid twice.

The bitch's owner should leave with a signed registration form for her hoped-for litter, and also a copy of the dog's pedigree. If your dog is popular and in demand, you will find it exhausting and time-consuming to copy each one by hand. Most people photocopy the original or have stud-cards printed. It is also a good idea to give the owner a copy of your dog's eye certificate and hip-score sheet.

I ask owners to inform me when their bitches whelp. I do this for two reasons: the first being to keep my records up to date; and the second to permit me to pass on any puppy enquiries I might receive.

One point I should like to make about the responsibility of the stud-dog owner is that if you ever permit poor specimens, or those without proof of heredity examinations, to be mated to your dog, then you are as guilty of malpractice as if you had bred the litter yourself. If all the stud-dog owners refused such bitches, there would be a considerable increase in soundness of stock. As I said at the beginning, dog-breeding is a serious and responsible business.

If your attempt at breeding Golden Retrievers falls short of your expectations, be completely honest with yourself and try to work out what went wrong. Perhaps that wonderful top dog who was so suitable for your bitch was less suitable than you thought. Perhaps your bitch, for all her clear eyes, sweet temperament and incredibly low hip-score, is just not good enough. You should strive to be your own greatest critic. The criticism of others may be coloured by envy; your own criticism should be the product of totally honest soul-searching. Each time you breed a litter it should be as good and, ideally, better than what came before. If this is not so, then re-appraise your ideas. Have in mind the Breed Standard at all times. Any deviation from this exhibited by your stock is a retrograde step. Your aim is progress. If you have this conviction coupled with dedication, you deserve to succeed.

9

Pregnancy and Whelping

Pregnancy

For the first month after mating, your bitch's diet need not alter. If she is receiving a good supply of protein, carbohydrate and minerals, then this will suffice for the time being. As soon as you can see quite definitely that she is in whelp, you can increase her diet.

There are various methods of detecting pregnancy. Some breeders notice the hair curling upwards over the couplings. Others see an obvious change in the shape of the rib-cage. One good sign is that the bitch's nipples will elongate and turn bright pink. The majority of bitches show they are in whelp by a change in their personality more than by a change in their appearance. Bitches who have formerly been 'tomboys' and very independent, suddenly behave impeccably and start to cling to their owners.

These methods might be reliable but remember that most of these signs manifest themselves in a very real manner for a false pregnancy too. Many breeders have, at some time, been quite positive that their bitches are in whelp, only to find as the day approaches, that they revert to normal in both behaviour and shape.

A much more reliable method is the use of an electronic scanner. With some of these, the puppies appear on the screen as vague outlines. Other machines produce a printed picture for the owner. This equipment is not infallible and most of us have heard tales about bitches pronounced 'empty' at the time of scanning, later going on to produce good-sized litters. These are in the minority; in most cases, the scanner is accurate. Sometimes the number of puppies being carried is difficult to define, especially when they lie one behind the other.

There is no need to feel apprehensive about using a scanner on your pregnant bitch as it is both harmless and painless. Sheep farmers have relied on scanners for their ewes for years. The whole procedure is over in a matter of minutes. The operator passes an

152

instrument not unlike a stethoscope over the bitch's abdomen and the picture appears on the screen.

Some breeders use such services as a matter of course. I do not because I so enjoy the excitement of the uncertainty attached to mating a bitch. I like trying to detect early signs, and it is my bitches' behaviour more than anything else which informs me they are pregnant. Having them scanned would deprive me of this.

Scanning has two great advantages: it informs you that you can start feeding your bitch extra rations, if she is in whelp; and it prevents your making her fat by extra feeding if she is not in whelp. Most of us have fed and fed a bitch only to find how unwise were our actions as the sixty-third day approached.

Diet and Exercise

Ideally, as soon as you are positive your bitch is pregnant, she should start having extra food divided into three meals a day. In theory, this sounds fine but so many of my bitches loathe the very sight of food from this stage onwards. One of my bitches, Thyra, vomited every morning of her pregnancy from the second week. By lunchtime she was prepared to eat a little food, usually scrambled eggs and brown bread. Then at teatime she would eat meat, but only after much persuasion. At bedtime she would accept two hard biscuits. The total volume of these meals was far less than she ate before she was mated. Her ten puppies were of normal size and were very healthy.

Another of my bitches ate steadily throughout her pregnancy. She never behaved as though she was pregnant, and insisted on regular walks, even on the day her puppies were born. Each day, she ate breakfast of cereal and milk, or hard biscuits and milk. At lunchtime, she had scrambled eggs and meal. For her late-afternoon meal she ate meat and biscuits and, before going to bed, a handful of dry biscuits. She also produced ten puppies, which were the same size as Thyra's.

My bitches all take free exercise when they are in whelp. Only in the last fortnight do I keep them on a lead for the start of their walks, to prevent their dashing ahead like lunatics and bumping into one another. For the second part of the walk I allow them to be free and by the time we are nearing home they are walking sedately at heel.

For the last fortnight before whelping they tend to become tired very easily and I encourage them to spend a lot of time resting, although that does not preclude chasing cows and stray cats when the opportunity arises. I find they often need to relieve themselves halfway through the night, so I set my alarm for around 4a.m. in order to let them out into the field.

Preparing your Bitch for Whelping

During the last week of pregnancy, I trim all the feathering off my bitch's tail and hind legs because over the years, my bitches have been prone to wet eczema on the underside of their tails and on the backs of their hind legs after whelping. My Golden Retrievers carry really dense coats and the natural discharge after whelping is absorbed by all this fur, which acts like a sponge. I can only imagine the discomfort felt by the bitch when puppies are climbing all over an area affected by wet eczema. In the past, I have tried to prevent this problem occurring by washing and drying my bitches carefully after whelping.

But I have found it far more effective to cut off this fur. Not only are my bitches free from eczema, but there is the added advantage that there is an absence of the smell associated with wet fur after whelping. Also, the hair does grow luxuriantly afterwards. The doubts expressed by other breeders – that removing the fur will lead to the puppies getting cold – I have found to be quite unfounded. My puppies are born in the house and I find they are always warm and comfortable. I use no extra heating but the central heating is, of course, on in the winter.

As the whelping day approaches, it is quite normal for a bitch to go off her food. Remember that in the wild she would eat all the afterbirths (and will now, given the chance), so she will be reluctant to fill herself up with other foods. Sometimes she will eat her usual food with great enthusiasm but will vomit immediately. As long as she has only brought up the meal and there is no particularly evil-smelling matter present, do not be alarmed, as this is a natural practice. She will also probably vomit after drinking water.

Golden Retrievers are wonderful excavators and they never dig larger holes than just before they whelp. This craze sometimes lasts as long as a month after they have whelped. There is no way of preventing this trait and only by physically restraining them can you stop them disappearing down a hole. So strong is the urge to dig that even the most obedient bitches become deaf when told not to do so.

You will know when your bitch is about to whelp because her expression will change and she will look far away and pre-occupied. Sometimes she will pant furiously and will attempt to make a bed with the carpet or her own rug. Her movements will be quite obsessive. There is no way you can miss it.

Most Golden Retrievers follow their owners around for a few days before whelping and simply refuse to let them out of their sight. Years ago, when I had my first Border Collie litter, I found the bitch's behaviour very strange by comparison: she wanted to be alone and then, during the actual whelping, she wanted me present but at a distance. She also resented any offer of help and would crowd over her puppies if I approached, even though she had the sweetest possible temperament, comparable to the best Golden Retriever.

Prepare your whelping-box in advance. All gestation tables tell us that bitches whelp sixty-three days after mating. However, all my bitches whelp on the sixtieth day. I have also had one produce a live litter on the fifty-sixth day and Sh.Ch. Linchael Heritage produced a still-born litter on the seventieth, with no apparent effort and no detrimental effect to herself. It will remain a mystery why these puppies were not born earlier as there was no obvious complication.

The whelping-box should be large enough for a bitch to lie down in comfortably, and should ideally have adjustable sides so that their height can be increased when necessary. Line the box with a proprietary brand of fleecy polyester fabric sold for the purpose. This fabric is used by veterinary surgeons because it is highly absorbent and washable. It is ideal for the whelping-box: the moisture goes through leaving the surface dry and it gives the pups an excellent footing. Although it becomes very stained in the process, I have never had a piece which did not revert to snowy white after washing. It will dry over a radiator in minutes. If you have several bitches, or could share with one or two friends, it is an excellent idea to buy a full roll from the manufacturers. You will find this will be a fraction of the cost of buying it by the piece.

I have frequently witnessed litters being whelped on newspaper. The bitches look miserable and the puppies are cold and wet. Newspaper forms into a nasty grey mass. It might be cheap but the sight of it is enough to make me doubly convinced of the virtues of the fleecy material as the perfect bedding for whelping.

It is a good idea to give your bitch a bath with a good insecticidal shampoo a fortnight before she whelps. Pay particular attention to the area around the teats, ensuring that this is thoroughly rinsed.

Worming of bitches that are to be bred from is very important if the puppies are to be as free from infestation as possible. I worm mine as soon as they come into season but I would like to adopt the practice of worming regularly throughout pregnancy. Those who use this method record great success with the freedom from infestation in the resulting litters.

Your bitch will have been well fed during her pregnancy. She will be tired but healthy as the day approaches. The whelping-box is ready, so now all you can do is sit back and wait for the moment to arrive.

Whelping

Most bitches pant furiously for as much as twenty-four hours before whelping. Others will give no signs at all. A good sign that whelping is imminent is when bitches drink after much panting, then immediately vomit. Often, this process is repeated many times before obvious contractions may be observed. This is the moment for her to occupy the whelping-box.

Contractions are a sign that the first puppy should be born quite soon, although there is no definite time limit. Some bitches will contract for a long time without producing a puppy. The contractions even become stronger and more rapid but then die away and appear to begin all over again. This does not necessarily mean anything is wrong. I remember reading all that was available on whelping before I had my first litter. Nearly every book stated that if the bitch strains for an hour and no puppy appears, then something must be wrong.

Years later, I have often wondered if this is the reason why so many puppies are born by Caesarean section. I do not advocate letting a bitch continue to contract for too long but neither am I in favour of being in too much of a hurry to involve the vet. If the contractions die away and do not return, I then call the vet as it is possible that uterine inertia has occurred, which makes further contractions impossible without help. At this stage the vet will administer an injection which should soon have her contracting.

Most bitches will look anxiously towards their tails as each contraction occurs. They will often turn in circles, frantically licking their vulvas. At this stage, there is often a dark-green discharge. The first whelping I attended, I was quite horrified by this colour but since then I have accepted it as an integral part of whelping. It does wash off the bitch and the bedding quite easily.

Soon after the discharge, as the bitch pushes, the first puppy begins to emerge. Most come head first, enclosed in a sac. Others come hindquarters first. This is called the breech position. Since the hindquarters are wider than the head and shoulders, the bitch will have to work harder with puppies presenting in this way. If the puppy seems firmly stuck, you can help by grasping it firmly behind the forelegs (if it is presented head first). Pull as the bitch pushes, but stop pulling as she relaxes. If the puppy is in a breech position grasp it around the waist and pull as before.

Most bitches will lie on their sides to whelp. This is by far the easiest position as far as the helper is concerned. Some will sit, which makes any observation of the birth impossible. Other bitches will stand, squat or even walk about. Ideally you should restrain your bitch and persuade her to lie on her side, which is sometimes easier in theory than in practice.

The puppies are usually born in fluid-filled sacs. Some bitches know exactly what is expected of them and immediately tear this sac with their teeth. If she does not perform this task, you must do it for her, tearing the membrane with your nails. There is no feeling in this sac, so your actions will not be felt by the puppy or the bitch.

The fluid contained in copious quantities in each sac can irritate your skin. Barrier cream helps protect human skin but vast quantities are needed if you take into account how often you need to wash your hands during whelping.

The puppy is attached to the afterbirth (placenta) by the umbilical cord. This mass will remain inside the bitch for a few minutes after the puppy is born. Do not pull in an effort to free it because you will risk causing a hernia. Using scissors, cut the cord about 1 inch (2.5 cm) from the puppy's stomach. This cord is full of the blood from which the puppy has been receiving nourishment for the last nine weeks. Obviously, some of this blood will remain in the cord and will be lost when you sever it. A little blood looks a lot when spilled on to a white blanket, but do not be alarmed. This will not be felt by the bitch or her puppy. If you leave a longer length of cord, the bitch will nearly always chew it to the length she prefers. Some bitches will chew the cord, so separating their pups from the placenta, before you have a chance to deal with it. This is perfectly acceptable and I allow the bitch to eat two or three placentas, before removing the rest. A few provide nourishment, but too many cause vomiting.

If the litter is a large one, the first puppies will get in the way of the next to be born. Have a hot-water bottle wrapped in a towel at the edge of the box. Some breeders place this in a separate box, but I find that while my bitches are quite willing to allow me to place their puppies at the side of the whelping box, they become demented if I remove them from their view. The puppies quickly settle on their warm bottle, so staying dry and permitting their mother to attend to the new arrival, without fear of crushing those already born.

The bitch will often be glad of a drink of milk half way through the whelping. If the whelping is very prolonged, I persuade the bitch to come outside and relieve herself. When you do this at night, take a torch with you, as many a bitch has squatted to relieve herself and has deposited a puppy on the grass as well. I spoke to one very distressed owner who had discovered a dead puppy in the garden the next morning. With a little forethought, most disasters are avoidable. If the bedding has become very wet and soiled, it is a good idea to have someone ready to change it while you are in the garden with the bitch.

It is very difficult for the novice owner to tell when a bitch has finished whelping, and reasonably difficult for the experienced breeder. The best way is to stand the bitch, then feel the abdomen, back inside the hind legs. I use the palms of my hands for this and am feeling for a puppy-shaped lump. Do not be confused by the uterus, which will have assumed unusual proportions during the pregnancy. It will feel lumpy, but a puppy will feel much harder than this, with the head like a small apple.

If you are reasonably sure she has finished, allow her to relieve herself, and change the bedding again. You will find she will only leave the whelping-box, on a collar and lead, with the utmost persuasion from you. Once outside, she will squat, then dash madly back to her puppies. Even the most sedate bitches break speed records to get back to their families.

Ensure she lies down gently when returning to them. Some are so keen to be with their puppies that they flop on top of them, unaware of any that might be trapped by their weight. Rails round the edges of the box should provide escape routes for any who would be trapped behind their mother. Most bitches show great care and will look around before lying down, nosing out of the way any in danger.

The problem with bitches lying on puppies can occur if they get restless during the first night. After whelping, some are so tired that they seem only half-conscious of what they are doing. It is in this tired state that they can go down on them. The only way you can prevent this happening is by being there. To spend the first two or three nights beside the litter is a sound arrangement. You can make yourself reasonably comfortable with a camp-bed and sleeping bag. I find I doze rather than sleep but am aware of the slightest sound from the puppies or their dam.

Care of the Bitch and Puppies

Bitches can, and often do, behave in the oddest way soon after whelping. Most Golden Retrievers are sweet and gentle and do not resent your presence or your handling of the puppies. Some crowd over their children if you interfere but this usually passes within a couple of days. It is essential that the bitch should have peace and quiet with the minimum disturbance. I do not permit visitors until the litter is at least a week old. By then, the bitches are usually back to normal and are proud to show off their families.

Other forms of odd behaviour are noticeable in newly whelped bitches. They will sometimes make beds in their whelping-boxes, so risking burying their pups. To prevent this happening, the bedding can be fixed under screwed-down wooden strips, which makes changing the bedding quite a chore, but the puppies are safe. Other bitches become obsessive about digging holes in the carpet. This behaviour may persist for several weeks but does pass eventually. Golden Retrievers are dedicated hole-diggers at the best of times but, when they whelp, this obsession tends to increase. After they have whelped the hole-diggers have a great need to inspect these holes every time they go out. If the weather is wet, this is a great nuisance since she will return dirty to her litter in a clean whelping-box.

Some bitches who have never been chewers will almost demolish the edges of the whelping-box within the first few days of whelping. I cannot imagine why they do this unless it is to alleviate the boredom of lying for hours with their pups. Certainly, it is the most active bitches who tend to do this. It is very irritating to have to hand-pick the tiny splinters from the bedding.

Where you whelp your bitches and then keep them with their families is largely a matter of choice. For years I sat for hours in my puppy-kennel. Now, my bitches whelp in the house, which is a far better place in my opinion, since everything I am likely to need is

159

there. A utility room is ideal, being away from the main rooms, yet within access of all facilities

For the first few days after whelping, very little needs to be done apart from changing soiled bedding and ensuring the puppies are warm enough. I never use any form of extra heating, other than a radiator in the whelping room. I find heat lamps that are warm enough to be of benefit to the puppies are too warm for their dams. When my puppies go out to the puppy-kennel at three weeks old, they have a wall-mounted, oil-filled radiator. This keeps them comfortable as may be seen from the way they sleep spread out. If they huddle one on top of the other, they are feeling cold and are attempting to conserve their body heat.

Most of the care in the beginning will be centred around your bitch. She will need taking out to relieve herself at four-hourly intervals, or more frequently if she demands. She will need to have a light diet initially, then plenty of food. For the first two days after whelping, give egg and milk as scrambled eggs, with brown bread or breakfast cereal. For the next two days, two of her four meals might comprise rabbit or chicken with brown bread. Towards the end of the first week, she should be having cooked minced meat for one meal and you should be starting to introduce her usual biscuit meal. By the end of the second week she should be having the following sort of menu:

07.30 a.m.   Rabbit or chicken with biscuit meal
12.00 a.m.   2 scrambled eggs with cereal or brown bread
 5.30 p.m.   Minced beef with biscuit meal
 9.30 p.m.   Breakfast cereal with milk

You can alternate biscuit meal with rice or pasta. This never causes diarrhoea, which can be a problem in a newly whelped bitch.

By the third week the bitch will be eating very large quantities of food and I generally feed as much as she demands. Occasionally, you will come across a bitch who is so greedy that demand-feeding is out of the question but, generally, Golden Retrievers know when they have had enough.

The time when you have to be extremely careful with your bitch's diet is when you start to wean the pups. She will then clean up after them and this sometimes gives rise to diarrhoea. Cut down the meat at this time and increase the carbohydrate. Rice and pasta keep the motions firm.

Bitches who have whelped show varying degrees of vaginal discharge. For the first few days it is bottle green. Then it is stringy and blood-tinged. From this time onwards, it grows paler but some form of discharge persists into the fifth week. If the colour changes dramatically, such as the pinkish discharge suddenly becoming very blood-stained, seek your vet's advice. He will probably administer a broad-spectrum antibiotic, which is usually followed by a ten-day course of tablets. Some breeders request such treatment for their bitches as a matter of course, but I am not a believer in the use of drugs until the need arises. The degree of discharge seems to bear no relation to the length or difficulty at the whelping and the bitches do not seem to be aware of it. The main problem is the way wagging tails can spread it around the room. Never was kitchen-roll put to better use! This discharge has an obvious, though not unpleasant, smell and I wash the bitch's trousers daily for the first week. They do not seem to mind having the hair-drier used on them at this time any more than they do normally. In fact, I have found that bitches who object to its use for show preparation, will submit quite readily to its use after whelping.

Do not make your bitch stay in the whelping-box all the time. They must be able to get away from their puppies and any attempt to force them to stay within range of all those demanding mouths all the time is tantamount to cruelty. Most bitches will start to leave the box after the first three days, lying beside it, chin over the edge, keeping a watchful eye on their charges. One of my bitches left the box after feeding them for the first time and only ever returned to feed and clean her puppies, yet in middle-age she became a sort of midwife who supervised the feeding of everyone else's pups and would join in with the cleaning process.

On the seventh day after whelping, cut the puppies' nails. They are very sharp and unless attended to weekly, will make the bitch thoroughly sore, which will lead to a reluctance to feed them. When doing this, you should be extremely careful to avoid cutting the quick, which will bleed if damaged. Only the white, chalky tips of the nails should be removed. I find human nail-clippers the most effective tool for this operation. Remember the tips of dew-claws too. I never have the whole dew-claws removed. Many breeders do, saying that it prevents possible injury later on, but I can truthfully say that none of my dogs has ever torn a dew-claw. I leave them intact for the same reason that prevents my having a breed that needs its tail docking.

Weaning

The process of weaning may be started as early as two weeks if the litter is a large one or left until three weeks if it comprises five puppies or less. The earlier the puppies' food is supplemented, the less strain there is on the bitch.

Begin by mixing up a quantity of baby cereal with puppy milk. The consistency is important: it should be halfway between runny and thick custard. If it is too thin, the puppies will cough as they start to lap. If it is too thick they will get a mass stuck to the roofs of their mouths.

To encourage the puppy to lap, gently dip the puppy's mouth in the mixture. The puppy's usual reaction is to blow bubbles, then to splutter, but once they have got the idea, nothing stops them. Use shallow dishes, or they will not be able to balance and get their chins over the edges. I use flat, sponge tins at this stage, with three puppies to a tin. Very soon they push and shove (and even walk across the centre), so I change to individual, shallow stainless-steel feeding bowls.

I start the weaning process just before the puppies go to bed for the night. Then I progress to a morning and an evening feed and before very long they are having four meals each day.

It is a good idea to arm yourself with a bowl of warm water, a face cloth and a towel for these feeding sessions, so that their faces may be cleaned. A few puppies are capable of spreading a bowl of cereal over a very wide area.

Quite soon after the puppies have started to lap the cereal mixture, they may be introduced to their first, solid feed. The best raw minced beef cannot be equalled as a starter. It is very rewarding to see the little blunt noses poking about at the mince one minute, unsure what to do with it, and then the next minute devouring it with such obvious enjoyment. The problem with introducing meat is that the puppies like it so much that they tend to be less keen on the cereal mixture.

It is almost impossible to state how much each puppy needs. If they eat with enthusiasm, look well rounded and glossy and there is no diarrhoea, you are doing it right. Little is as reassuring to the breeder than seeing a litter eating well, then immediately passing firm motions. Diarrhoea is a sure sign that all is not well with your feeding programme. If you mix the milk powder rather too strongly it is certain that diarrhoea will result. The motions will also be loose if you make any sudden change in the diet. The rule is to proceed with caution when feeding puppies. What you might consider to be a slight change in their diet, could have a devastating result.

If you intend feeding a complete puppy food, follow the manufacturer's instructions to the letter. You will not be helping by adding anything to this balanced food as it will contain everything the puppy requires.

By four weeks, I allow the bitches to return to their puppies after I have fed them, if they choose to do so. At this time, the puppies have had the edge taken from their appetites by their recent meal, so are a little kinder to the bitch. You can gradually reduce her visits to one in the morning and one last thing at night. By five weeks she will be sleeping away from them at night.

When your bitch is feeding the puppies at the three- to four-week stage, watch for signs of eclampsia. This condition is caused by a reduced calcium level in her blood and will cause total collapse and death if unattended. If you suspect eclampsia, call the vet immediately. A calcium injection brings about a miraculous recovery and she will be on her feet within minutes.

When the puppies are five weeks old, I do not allow them to have their mother with them at night any more. If she wishes to return to them during the day, I permit this, but I do not persuade her to do so. By this time they are all eating heartily and can last from their late-night feed until breakfast. Most bitches are relieved to leave their boisterous families by this time and move back into the house with no signs of concern. There are bitches who exhibit signs of stress at leaving them for the first time but I find a couple of night visits soon reassures them that no harm is befalling their puppies and they are then happy to settle in the house again.

I bath all my pupppies at least twice before they go to their new homes. However cleanly you keep them, it is always possible for them to pick up a parasitic infestation. Several times I have been approached by new breeders who are upset to find their puppies have obvious signs of infestation. They feel ashamed and protest that they have always kept the litter clean. There is no need to feel embarrassed, just a need to ensure that precautions are taken in the future. Two baths are needed, one to kill the parasites, and another ten to fourteen days later to kill the hatching eggs. There are shampoos specifically for this purpose but care must be taken that they are suitable for young puppies. Be guided by your veterinary surgeon.

The best place to bath puppies is in the kitchen sink. Ensure that the water is not too hot, remembering that dogs cannot tolerate temperatures anywhere near as high as those tolerated by us. The draining-board is a good drying area. It should be covered with a thick towel to stop the puppies' feet sliding about. I towel dry, then use a hair-drier. Most puppies are initially a little surprised by the stream of air but soon become accustomed to it.

At this time, your new puppy owners will want to visit and choose. Invite them to arrive midway between meals as this is when the puppies are at their most active. Once a puppy has been chosen, that puppy needs to be marked to distinguish it from the rest. Some breeders use an indelible marker. I prefer to clip off tiny sections of fur and then enter records of this in a book. These entries read: 'Left hind leg of puppy bitch – Mr Smith'. The clipped patch soon grows but remains sufficiently obvious for identification purposes.

It is important to keep records of each litter. I use a hardbacked book for the purpose. Record the names of sire and dam and the date the puppies were born. Then list their registered names and also the names and addresses of their new owners. It is also a good idea to list their Kennel Club registration numbers: this is invaluable when new owners misplace these certificates and need to contact you for replacements.

I positively encourage all my puppy owners to keep in contact with me. At first, they tend to get in touch if things go wrong but eventually it settles to a card-at-Christmas relationship. Some have remained good friends for over twenty years. The provision of an after-sales service is an essential part of being a breeder. I feel responsible for my puppies throughout their lives and inform the new owners that if, for any reason, they cannot keep them, I will welcome them back. This has happened twice in almost thirty years.

10

Ailments and Diseases

by Dr Larry Roberts MRCVS

It is not possible to cover fully all the diseases which might occur in the individual pet dog or in the breeder's stock. Therefore emphasis has been placed on common conditions which may be encountered by both the pet owner and the breeder, either with one or two bitches or a large kennel.

It is important to establish a good working relationship with your veterinary surgeon, based on mutual respect. You should have confidence in the advice and services offered by your vet, and in turn your vet should respect your experience and knowledge of dogs. Establishment of such a rapport will help in maintaining good health in your dogs, whether you have a single pet dog or a larger kennel. As a sympathetic owner you will know your dogs well and changes in behaviour, appetite, drinking habits, etc. should alert you as to whether or not something is amiss. Regular grooming is an important part of skin care, and it is useful once a week, as part of the grooming session, to give your dogs a check over. Turn back the gums and examine the teeth, build up of tartar can be a problem in some dogs with resultant gum recession. If there is excessive tartar build-up, it is a relatively simple task for your veterinary surgeon to remove this. Eyes should be examined, excessive tear production with staining would indicate that all is not well and may warrant veterinary attention. Ears can easily be checked and in some dogs excessive wax production is common. There are proprietary products available for cleaning the ears by dissolving the wax. During grooming you should run your hands over the dog's body to check for any abnormalities. By doing this you should be able to detect injuries which have possibly gone unnoticed, or growths, which can then be monitored and brought to the attention of your vet at the next visit (unless rapid growth or ulceration indicates that more immediate attention is warranted). As dogs age, such growths develop more frequently and timely surgical intervention can be beneficial.

In addition to the early detection of problems, this weekly once-over will allow you to assess the condition of your dog. You should be able to make out individual ribs, not rolls of fat when running your hands over the chest, but it is important not to assume that a dog is fat just because he has a heavy coat, or that a thin dog is necessarily a fit dog. Know your dog and feed to maintain ideal body condition. Requirements will vary not only from dog to dog, but in individual dogs at various times.

If you have worries or queries, contact your veterinary surgeon who may be able to give reassurance and advice on the telephone, or suggest that a visit to the surgery for examination is indicated.

Specific Infections

The most important infectious conditions are now controlled by effective vaccination programmes. These conditions include the viral diseases: distemper, infectious canine hepatitis and canine parvovirus; and the bacterial infections: *Leptospira canicola* and *Leptospira icterohaemorrhagiae*. All dogs should be vaccinated against these infections. Additional vaccines are also available against two of the agents implicated in kennel cough: canine parainfluenza virus and *Bordetella bronchiseptica*.

Kennel Cough

A number of agents have been implicated in kennel cough including the bacterium *Bordetella bronchiseptica*, and various viruses.

In kennel cough, coughing usually develops five to ten days after contact with an infected animal. Such contact most often occurs at shows or in boarding kennels. The animal may remain bright and alert, have a good appetite and the soft dry cough may be the only sign. Coughing spasms may develop.

Veterinary attention should be sought so that the appropriate antibiotic therapy can be started. Prompt treatment can reduce the duration of the illness. This is a highly contagious condition and contact with other dogs should be avoided if your dog or kennel is affected.

Endoparasites

A number of internal parasites affect dogs including roundworms (*Toxocariasis*) and tapeworms (*Dipylidium* and *Taenia*). Since *Toxocariasis* can present a risk to human health and all dogs are infected, it will be considered in detail.

Roundworms

Toxocara canis   This roundworm is very common in dogs, and its life cycle will be considered to show the reasons for this, and to explain why its control can present difficulties.

Eggs are passed in the faeces of infected animals, and require a period of development (maturation) before they are infective – this may be as short as three to four weeks under optimum conditions (as in mid-summer), but may take months in winter. When eaten by a dog, the eggs hatch in the intestine and the larvae migrate via the bloodstream to the liver, then to the lungs. The larvae then return to the intestines via the trachea and become egg-laying adults. This is the main route of migration in dogs up to three months of age; over this age, most of the larvae remain in the bloodstream rather than enter the lungs, and they are distributed widely in tissues throughout the body. In adult dogs, the majority of larvae become dormant in body tissues. An exception is the bitch around whelping when migration via the lungs to the intestine takes place again.

Prenatal infection occurs from about the forty-second day of pregnancy when a proportion of the dormant larvae become reactivated and cross the placenta to develop in the foetuses. An infected bitch will usually have sufficient dormant larvae to infect all her litters. A few of the reactivated larvae in the bitch will pass via the lungs to the intestines so resulting in an increase in *Toxocara* egg excretion by the bitch in the weeks following whelping. The suckling puppies can also become infected through larvae in the bitch's milk during the first three weeks of life.

In addition, rodents and birds can become infected if they ingest the *T. canis* eggs. The larvae remain dormant in these hosts until eaten by a dog when development resumes.

Toxocaris leonina   This worm is similar to the *Toxocara canis* roundworm and is also common in dogs, buts its life cycle is less complex and does not involve extensive migration through the tissues of the

167

dog, so that infection through milk or across the placenta does not occur. Infection takes place following ingestion of eggs from the environment or through eating prey animals with larvae in their tissues.

Heavy burdens of *T. canis* or *T. leonina* can have a marked effect in puppies: puppies up to two weeks old have nasal discharge, noisy breathing and poor growth; puppies of three to four weeks may exhibit vomiting and diarrhoea and retarded growth; puppies of six to twelve weeks have pale mucous membranes, a pot-bellied appearance and chronic diarrhoea.

Control of roundworm infections is difficult for a number of reasons. The complex life cycle has already been outlined; but an additional problem is that the eggs are long lived, stick to surfaces very effectively and are resistant to disinfection. Good hygiene and scrubbing with large volumes of hot water will help to reduce the egg numbers in concrete runs.

Strategic use of wormers (anthelmintics) is essential to control this problem, and a number of effective products are available. The main part of the pup's worm burden is acquired before birth or via the milk and it would seem logical to control infection by eliminating the tissue larvae in the bitch. Wormers are available which will prevent infection across the placenta and via the milk, but they need to be given daily for two to three weeks before whelping and two to three weeks afterwards.

Control is commonly exercised by the routine treatment of nursing bitches and puppies using anthelmintics which remove worms from the intestines. In addition to preventing disease in the puppies, it also reduces contamination of the environment with eggs, and hence reduces the risk to succeeding litters. Recommended intervals of dosing vary but an optimum programme would be to treat puppies weekly from two weeks of age up to weaning, then every two weeks up to three months old and then again at six months. Although adult dogs are likely to carry few worms it is recommended that they should be dosed twice yearly.

Tapeworms

Dipylidium caninum   This tapeworm can infect both dogs and cats, and its life cycle involves fleas (or occasionally lice). The freshly passed segments of this worm resemble rice grains. They are mobile and crawl about on the tail region of the dog. For further development the egg has to be ingested by a larval flea (or louse). The dog becomes infected when the flea is swallowed while he is grooming himself. Effective anthelmintics are available for treating *D. caninum* infection but control of the ectoparasites is also essential.

Taenia spp.   These are unlikely to cause clinical problems in the dog. They are parasites that affect meat animals such as sheep, cattle, pigs, rabbits and hares, and will only be encountered by a dog if he is fed uncooked meat and offal. Effective drugs for removal of these tapeworms are available.

Ectoparasites

A variety of external parasites can affect dogs. Control of such parasites is extremely important.

Fleas

The most common flea found on dogs is the cat flea, the dog flea being less usual. Rabbit and hedgehog fleas may also occur on dogs if they have contact with these animals. Fleas cause irritation and itching, but, in a percentage of dogs, hypersensitivity to flea saliva develops causing a severe allergic reaction. Since flea dirt is made up of dried blood, the presence of black flecks indicates flea infestation.

Fleas spend most of their life cycle off the host. This includes not only the eggs and larvae but also the adults, which can survive off the host for as long as six months between feeds. Control will therefore depend on treatment of the dog with an insecticide and also the dog's bed, blankets and immediate environment. Effective sprays and shampoos are easily obtainable.

Lice

The lice most commonly found on dogs are the sucking lice and these can occasionally be a problem in kennels. They cause itching around the head and neck, and anaemia in puppies. The life cycle is completed on the dog and treatment with an insecticide should be effective in controlling them. Treatment needs to be repeated at an interval of fourteen days to kill newly hatched lice.

Mange

Sarcoptes, Demodex and Cheyletiella mange mites may all infect dogs.

Sarcoptic Mange (Scabies)   Sarcoptic mange causes intense skin irritation and particularly affects the ears, muzzle, face and elbows. In dogs kept in close contact, it spreads rapidly from dog to dog, so that in addition to treating the affected dog, it is necessary to treat any other dogs who share the environment.

Demodectic Mange   Demodex mites are found on the hair follicles. These mites are present on most dogs in low numbers, but in some cases, for reasons that are not understood, Demodex mites multiply causing skin damage without irritation. Defects in the immune system may be responsible for their sudden increase, and a hereditary susceptibility has been suggested. Owing to the deep-seated position of the mite, transmission does not occur easily. It is thought that pups acquire the mites early in life while suckling from the bitch. Treatment can be difficult, but newer compounds offer better control.

Cheyletiella   These mites live on the hairs, and only visit the skin to feed. The mites cause little damage to the dog's skin but rather give rise to marked skin scaling and varying degrees of itching. The condition is highly contagious. Treatment with an insecticidal shampoo is usually effective.

It should be borne in mind that Sarcoptic and Cheyletiella mange mites are transmissible to human skin resulting in skin irritation.

Skin Conditions

The skin is an important indicator of the health status of a dog. Confusion often arises in the area of skin disease due to the use of terms borrowed from human medicine such as eczema and dermatitis. Dermatitis is inflammation of the skin, irrespective of the cause. Eczema is inflammatory changes in the skin which are superficial and characterized by weeping, oozing and crusting. Both terms are non-specific, but describe inflammatory conditions which can arise from a variety of causes. This is a feature of skin problems: similar changes may have a variety of causes, including hormonal imbalance, ectoparasites, fungal infections (ringworm), dietary deficiency and hypersensitivity.

Allergic skin conditions may be due to contact hypersensitivity or food hypersensitivity, but the commonest cause is atopy. Atopy occurs when the dog becomes sensitized to inhaled substances, such as pollen. It has a genetic basis and it is more common in bitches than in dogs. The Golden Retriever is one of the breeds in which it occurs most frequently. Specialized diagnostic techniques are required to confirm the presence of such allergic disorders so that appropriate therapy can be implemented.

Alimentary Tract Diseases

Vomiting and diarrhoea are the most common signs associated with alimentary tract diseases. If signs of vomiting and diarrhoea occur but the dog remains alert and bright, it may be that all that is required to overcome the problem is to restrict food intake and to feed a bland diet such as scrambled eggs, custard or rice. If, however, the dog is dull and depressed, passing blood, retching or straining, then veterinary attention should be sought. If symptoms have persisted for some time, veterinary support will again be needed to identify the cause of the problem.

The vomiting reflex is well developed in the dog, since wild dogs feed their young by the regurgitation of food. This ability to vomit readily is advantageous in that it allows the removal of potentially damaging material. Vomiting can be caused by a variety of conditions, such as gastritis (inflammation of the stomach lining), foreign bodies, tumours in the stomach and intestines, and congenital conditions such as megaoesophagus (*see* page 175).

Diarrhoea can occur along with vomiting, as in gastro-enteritis, or it may be the sole indication of alimentary dysfunction. Diarrhoea is an increase in the frequency of passing stools and/or increased fluidity of the stool. The normal for any dog can vary and will depend on factors such as diet and temperament. Nutritionally induced diarrhoea is the commonest form of diarrhoea in the dog, and since sudden changes in diet can cause it, new diets should be introduced gradually.

Chronic Diarrhoea

Chronic diarrhoea is a common problem and results in weight loss. When diarrhoea is persistent, it may be necessary to carry out further investigations to establish the underlying reason. There are a number of recognized causes: exocrine pancreatic insufficiency, in which there are degenerative changes in the part of the pancreas responsible for producing enzymes involved in digestion; dietary sensitivity, for instance, to gluten, a substance present in wheat and almost all cereals except rice (commercial gluten-free diets are available to control this condition) and small intestinal bacterial overgrowth due to an increase in the numbers of bacteria present in the upper small intestine.

If the cause of diarrhoea in your dog is unclear, or if the condition is persistent, you should consult your vet.

Infections

Bacteria may cause clinical problems in puppies, but are less likely to do so in adults. In adult dogs, many cases described as bacterial enteritis are due to an alteration in the balance between commensal (normally present and harmless) bacteria, and harmful bacteria triggered off by other factors, usually dietary. However, certain bacteria can cause diarrhoea and these include *Campylobacter* and *Salmonella*. The latter is very rare, but *Campylobacter* infection is seen more often, although it is also uncommon.

Of the viral infections, parvovirus and coronavirus are the commonest. Parvovirus can cause a severe enteritis, but effective vaccines are available. Coronavirus appears to be common and produces a mild, short-lasting diarrhoea.

Diseases Associated with the Reproductive Tract and Breeding

Eclampsia (Hypocalcaemia)

Eclampsia is caused by low levels of calcium in the bloodstream and occurs most commonly in the three weeks after whelping, but may occur in late pregnancy, or during parturition. Symptoms are anxiety, restlessness and nervousness, followed within hours by

172

spasms and coma. The bitch may be panting excessively, irritable and have muscle tremors. Prompt veterinary treatment with calcium administered intravenously is necessary. After treatment, recovery is usually very fast.

Retained Placenta

When attending the whelping, it may be apparent to the owner that all the placentas have not been expelled from the uterus. Veterinary attention should be sought so that appropriate therapy to remove the retained foetal membranes can be applied. Antibiotic treatment is also indicated.

However, bitches with retained placentas may not be noticed until two or three days after whelping, when they may be dull, off their food and have a persistent green/brown discharge. Prompt veterinary attention is indicated.

Post-Partum Metritis

Infection of the uterus (womb) may occur following retained placenta or as a result of trauma at whelping. The bitch will have a smelly brown discharge from the vulva, be depressed, inappetant and have a raised temperature. Prompt veterinary attention is indicated. There may be a concurrent mastitis.

Post-Partum Haemorrhage

A blood-stained vulval discharge is normal after whelping, but the amounts of blood are usually small. If the blood in the discharge is excessive, veterinary attention should be sought to attempt to arrest the haemorrhage. Occasionally a hysterectomy is needed.

Mastitis

Infection can be introduced into the mammary tissue during the suckling period. One or more glands may be involved and those affected will be hard and hot. The bitch may be off-colour, inappetant and, if several glands are affected, the litter may be restless and require milk supplementation. Prompt veterinary attention and antibiotic therapy is required.

Pyometra

Pyometra is a common disease in the middle-aged and older bitch, but is occasionally seen in young bitches. It is caused by an accumulation of fluid in the uterus and most commonly occurs during the metoestrus phase of the oestrus cycle, i.e. the period after ovulation, which usually lasts for six to ten weeks. Bitches with pyometra may have a variety of symptoms: inappetance, excessive thirst, increased urination, vomiting and abdominal distension. In open pyometra, there will be vaginal discharge, which can vary in colour from cream to dark brown. There is no vaginal discharge in closed pyometra. Surgical removal of the uterus (hysterectomy) is indicated.

Cryptorchidism

At birth, the testes of the dog are positioned in the abdomen. When the puppy is seven to ten days old, they descend into the scrotum. In some puppies, they may be palpated by two weeks of age, and without difficulty by six to eight weeks.

Cryptorchidism is the condition where an animal has one or both testes retained at a site along the route of descent. It is an inherited condition, and treatment to induce descent should not be carried out. Surgical removal of any retained testicles is advisable, as there is an increased risk of development of tumours in retained testes.

Fading Puppy Syndrome

Puppies suffering from this syndrome are apparently healthy at birth but die within the first ten to fourteen days of life. This is a complex area and a number of factors can be involved. Congenital defects, infections (viral and bacterial), worm (ascarid) infections, mismanagement of the whelping and lactating bitch, and hypothermia (reduced body temperature) may all be involved.

If losses occur, it is important for your veterinary surgeon to examine the dam, the premises and obtain a full history of the bitch and kennel to try to assess which factors are involved in the losses. Detailed post-mortem examinations and microbiological testing will also be necessary.

Juvenile Cellulitis (Head-Gland Disease, Puppy Strangles)

This condition occurs in puppies from three weeks to twelve months of age, but is usually seen in puppies under four months old. It is not uncommon for several puppies in a litter to be affected. The condition starts with swelling of the head, particularly involving the lips. The skin becomes hard and reddened and the eyes and ears discharge. The lymph glands of the head and neck become enlarged and swollen and may rupture.

Early treatment by a veterinary surgeon is recommended to prevent scarring as both antibiotic and steroid therapy are required. The underlying basis for this condition appears to be a defect in immunity.

Megaoesophagus

Congenital megaoesophagus is the condition where the oesophagus is distended and in which there is a failure of the progressive synchronized movement of food along the oesophagus. The condition has been described in a number of breeds including the Golden Retriever and appears to have a hereditary basis.

One problem with this condition is that although some affected dogs may exhibit regurgitation/vomiting at weaning, not all affected dogs show clinical signs and in many dogs the condition has resolved itself by four to six months of age. This means that affected dogs may be used in the breeding programme as they clinically appear normal.

Once the condition is suspected, veterinary advice is needed and special (fluoroscopic) radiographic examination is needed to confirm the diagnosis. Feeding from an elevated bowl so that the head is higher than the stomach is a useful treatment. Frequent feeding of small quantities of moist food is also indicated.

Ectopic Ureter/Wet Puppies

This is the most common congenital defect of the ureters (the tubes carrying urine from the kidney to the bladder). As a result of faulty development, one or both ureters open somewhere other than into the bladder – usually the vagina in the bitch, and the urethra (the tube from the bladder to the exterior) in the dog. Fewer cases are reported in males and, in bitches, incontinence is invariably apparent from an early age, whereas in dogs it may appear much later in life, up to two-and-a-half years old. Incontinence is not seen in all affected dogs, and is sometimes intermittent and may be related to recumbency.

For confirmation of the presence of ectopic ureter, excretory urography is necessary, i.e. injection of a dye which is excreted through the kidneys and can be visualized on X-ray.

This condition is thought to be inherited, probably in a complex polygenic manner.

Epilepsy

Epilepsy is the condition in which recurrent fits occur. There is an abnormal electrical discharge in the brain which leads to the signs referred to as fits or convulsions. Fits caused by demonstrable causes are referred to as acquired or secondary epilepsy. When there is no demonstrable cause, the condition is idiopathic (primary) epilepsy. In dogs with idiopathic epilepsy there is a lower threshold at which fits are triggered by electrical impulses and these dogs are more susceptible to having fits. It is strongly suggested that idiopathic epilepsy occurs in the Golden Retriever.

In idiopathic epilepsy, fits commence at one to three years of age, although they have been described as early as six months and as late as six years old. The seizures are typically generalized, with paddling movements of the limbs, muscle tremors, jaw movements, salivation, defecation and urination. Most often they occur when the dog is sleeping or resting. Many owners notice altered behaviour in their dogs, such as restlessness or the exaggerated showing of affection for a variable period from minutes up to forty-eight hours before a seizure. After a fit, most dogs remain disorientated and have difficulty moving for a period that may last from minutes to hours. After recovery a voracious appetite and sleepiness are very often reported.

Owners with a 'fitting dog' should seek veterinary advice to eliminate possible secondary causes, as it is only by doing this that idiopathic epilepsy can be diagnosed. Appropriate anticonvulsant therapy can also be provided.

Hypothyroidism

Hypothyroidism is usually seen in the medium-sized and larger breeds and is quite common in Golden Retrievers. It results from an inadequate level of thyroid hormone. Most often dogs are affected in middle age (four to eight years).

Dogs with hypothyroidism can exhibit a wide range of signs. Prominent signs are lethargy, obesity and loss of hair. Veterinary advice is needed to confirm the diagnosis with appropriate laboratory tests and to institute corrective therapy.

Eye Conditions

Cataract

Cataract is the term applied to any opacity of the lens. The lens is situated behind the coloured part of the eye (the iris) and is transparent, lacking nerve and blood supply. It focuses light received into the eye onto the retina at the back of the eye where the light-sensitive receptors are located. Cataracts can affect one or both eyes, be partial or total, progressive or non-progressive. The part of the lens involved can vary, and assessment of the position of the cataract can be made using slit-light ophthalmoscopic equipment. Cataract can be present at birth, it can develop in puppies, in adult dogs or in ageing dogs.

There are a number of causes: trauma with injury to the eye involving the lens, toxic factors, dietary deficiencies, systemic diseases such as diabetes, and other eye diseases may result in cataract development. Hereditary cataracts are seen in a number of breeds including the Golden Retriever, and is mostly seen in young dogs although it occasionally develops in older dogs. In the Golden Retriever hereditary cataract is thought to be due to a dominant gene with incomplete penetrance. The cataract is situated at the back of the lens, and is most commonly a small non-progressive opacity, which has no effect on vision. However, less commonly it is progressive and eventually the whole lens becomes affected and the dog is blind at eighteen to twenty-four months old. Both forms are thought to be expressions of the same dominant gene.

Nuclear Sclerosis

Cataract should not be confused with senile nuclear sclerosis, which is a hardening of the lens occurring with age. It is due to the lens fibres, which are formed throughout life, becoming packed closer together in the centre of the lens. This gives the dog a greyish look within the pupil, and is not a cataract.

Progressive Retinal Atrophy

Progressive retinal atrophy (PRA) is an inherited eye condition in which the light-sensitive layer at the back of the eye (the retina) is gradually destroyed resulting in blindness. Ophthalmoscopic examination allows the disease to be divided into two main forms, generalized PRA and central PRA, different forms occurring in different breeds. Central PRA is the form encountered in the Golden Retriever, and in this condition many small pigment spots cover the retina, but blindness may not be total. At first, only the central part of the retina is involved but gradually the area involved increases so that virtually the whole retina is affected.

Signs are unlikely to be seen before one year of age. Vision is often better in dull rather than in bright light, such as sunlight, and is better peripherally than centrally. Affected dogs are able to detect moving objects in their visual field, but may fail to see quite large objects placed directly in front of them. If called from a distance, they may approach in an arc, and may walk past the owner without seeing him until they are almost level. Unlike generalized PRA, central PRA does not progress inevitably to total blindness, in fact, total blindness is uncommon.

Entropion

Entropion is the inturning of the eyelid and may affect the upper or lower eyelid or both; one or both eyes may be involved. It is considered to be an inherited condition although the mode of inheritance is unclear. Irritation of the front of the eye (the cornea) occurs and there is persistent tear staining. It can be first recognized when the dog is from a few weeks to several months old. Simple surgical correction is needed, but in young dogs it is better to delay surgery until maturity unless there is corneal damage.

BVA/KC Eye Scheme

The British Veterinary Association/Kennel Club eye scheme is designed to control and eradicate hereditary eye disease in those breeds with problems. In the Golden Retriever, it is applicable for PRA and hereditary cataract. PRA appears to be rare, but hereditary cataract occurs more commonly. Dogs should be examined annually from twelve months of age until death. Dogs should be used at stud and bitches bred from only if they have current clear eye certificates. Owners with multiple dogs should have all stock examined annually, even after they are no longer used for breeding, since, as already mentioned, hereditary cataract can appear for the first time very late in life. Examination of the eyes is undertaken by members of the Eye Scheme panel, made up of veterinary surgeons with the Certificate in Veterinary Ophthalmology (*see* Appendix 3, page 238).

One drawback to the scheme is that it cannot predict the development of changes later in life (which occurs in a small number of dogs) by which time, the dogs may already have been used for breeding. However it is essential that we all support the scheme to as full an extent as possible, only breeding from clear stock, and having our stock examined regularly and acting on the results.

Osteochondritis Dissecans (OCD)

This condition is seen in a number of medium-sized and large breeds including the Golden Retriever. A number of joints can be affected: shoulder, elbow, stifle and hock. In the Golden Retriever, it is commonly the elbow-joint. Within a joint, the two surfaces of the adjacent bones are covered in a smooth cartilaginous substance, the articular cartilage. In OCD, a flap of articular cartilage separates from the underlying bone.

Signs are usually first noticed between four and eight months of age, and the condition is more common in dogs than in bitches. Intermittent lameness of insidious onset, often worsening after exercise and with stiffness after rest should be investigated by a veterinary surgeon, who will, if appropriate, carry out an X-ray examination. Surgical treatment may be indicated.

The cause of the condition is unclear, although rapid growth rate is thought to play an important part. Overfeeding and excessive exercise have been suggested to play a role. A genetic component to the disease is being increasingly proposed. Current evidence indicates that the condition is inherited in a multifactorial way with both environmental factors and the additive effect of many genes being involved.

Hip Dysplasia

Hip dysplasia is an abnormal development of the hip-joint, influenced by hereditary and other factors. The hip-joint is referred to as a ball-and-socket joint, the rounded head of the femur fitting into the cup-like acetabulum. Hip dysplasia results in instability of the joint due to alterations of the head of the femur and a shallowness of the acetabulum. The degree of change can vary from slight to so severe that the head of the femur can become totally dislocated. The dog's movement does not always give an accurate assessment of the degree of hip dysplasia. Dogs with changes of hip dysplasia will develop osteoarthritis later in life.

In young dogs (less than one year old), hip dysplasia is usually characterized by either a swaying gait when walking or suddenly developing hind-leg stiffness after exercise. These latter dogs have difficulty in rising, and are reluctant to climb steps or stairs. Older dogs usually develop osteoarthritis following hip dysplasia and these dogs show stiffness, especially first thing in the morning (exaggerated if there has been vigorous exercise on the previous day). The stiffness eases as the dog moves. The clinical signs may be suggestive of hip dysplasia, but X-ray confirmation is necessary.

It is widely accepted that hip dysplasia is controlled by several genes, i.e. it is polygenic in character and the visible expression is a result of genetic and environmental factors. Dr Willis, using data from the BVA/KC Hip Dysplasia Scheme has estimated the heritability of hip dysplasia in the Golden Retriever to be 18 per cent. Despite the scepticism of some breeders, it is widely agreed that the heritability of hip dysplasia is significant and that stock with good hips will, in general, produce offspring with good hips.

Some other factors of importance in hip dysplasia are age, growth rate, weight, and exercise. Regarding age, dogs are born with normal hips and with increasing age the changes of hip dysplasia become more apparent. Although dogs can have hip dysplasia prior to twelve months of age, it is considered in the UK that X-ray diagnosis of hip dysplasia is generally not possible under twelve months old. Animals

X-rayed prior to this would need to be reassessed after they are a year old. In America, the Orthopaedic Foundation for Animals (OFA) have a lower age limit of two years old for hip-X-ray screening under their scheme.

BVA/KC Hip Dysplasia Scheme

Many schemes to control hip dysplasia are in operation throughout the world, and in some countries there are restrictions on breeding based on hip status. Using these programmes in certain countries, a significant improvement has been made in reducing hip dysplasia. Attempts have been made by the FCI (Federation Cynologique Internationale) to produce an international, unified standard. It is generally accepted that the BVA/KC standard is stricter than any other in Europe.

Under the BVA/KC Scheme, the hips of dogs are X-rayed when they reach twelve months of age or older. A general anaesthetic is required, but this is a safe, routine procedure and no longer carries the same risks that it did many years ago. The plates are then submitted to the BVA and a panel of expert veterinary radiographers (with the Diploma in Veterinary Radiography) assess and score these plates. It is the scoring of hip X-rays which is the basis for the scheme and it involves assessing nine parameters in relation to the hip, each hip being scored independently. The features scored are:

Norberg angle
Subluxation
Cranial acetabular edge
Dorsal acetabular edge
Cranial effective acetabular rim
Acetabular fossa
Caudal acetabular edge
Femoral head/neck exostosis
Femoral head recontouring

A number of these features are illustrated on the X-ray shown on page 182.

Norberg Angle If a line is drawn between the centres of the femoral heads and a second line between the centre of the femoral head and the cranial effective acetabular rim (*see* below), the angle

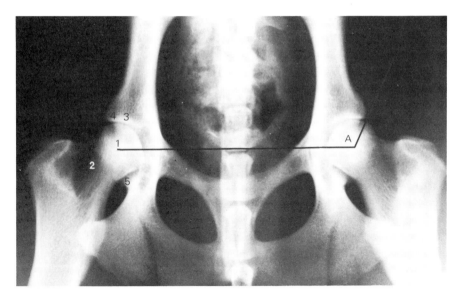

Fig 1 X-ray showing a 0:0 hip-score. The femoral head is
rounded and fits well into the acetabulam. There is no distortion
of the femoral head or extoses.   A Norberg Angle   1 Femoral head
2 Femoral neck   3 Cranial acetabular edge
4 Cranial effective acetabular rim   5 Caudal acetabular edge

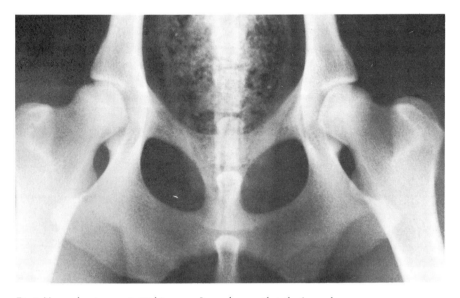

Fig 2 X-ray showing an 8:10 hip-score. It can be seen that the femoral
head does not fit as well into the acetabulum when compared with the
previous dog. This dog shows changes consistent with mild hip
dysplasia. This is the average score for the breed at this time.

182

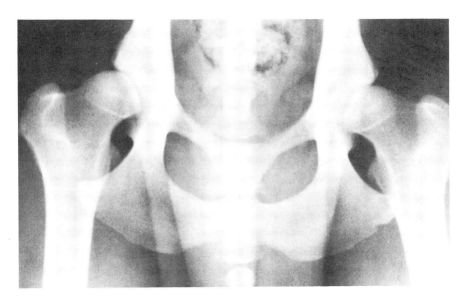

Fig 3 X-ray showing a 30:30 hip-score. There is a flattening
of the femoral head and thickening of the femoral neck. The head
fits poorly into the acetabular socket compared with the previous two
dogs. The acetabulum is much shallower. This dog shows changes
consistent with marked hip dysplasia.

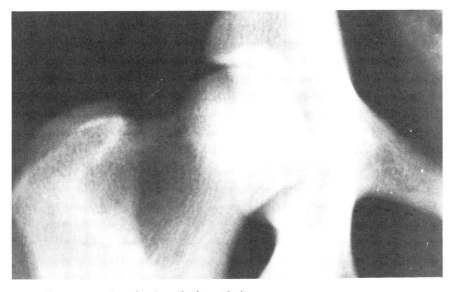

Fig 4 Close-up view of one hip from the dog with the
0:0 hip-score. This should be compared with the figure of a hip from
the dog with the 30:30 hip-score. The differences are obvious.

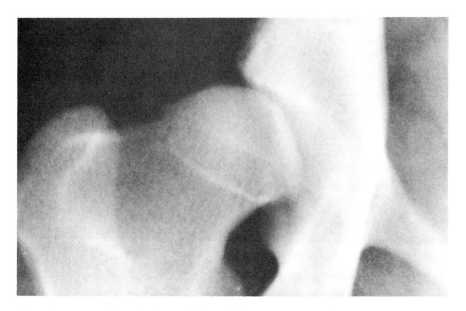

Fig 5 Close-up view of one hip from the dog with the
30:30 hip score. The difference in shape of the femoral head and
degree of fit into the acetabular head is apparent.

between these lines is the Norberg angle. The angle should be at least
105 degrees. This allows a measurement of the degree of dislocation
of the joint: the less the angle, the greater the dislocation.

Subluxation Subluxation is the term used to describe partial
dislocation of a joint, i.e. in the case of the hip-joint, the degree to
which the femoral head is separated from the lining of its socket, the
lining of the acetabulum. The greater the degree of hip dysplasia, the
greater will be the separation of the femoral head and acetabulum.

Cranial Acetabular Edge The cranial acetabular edge is the upper
curve of the acetabulum as seen on an X-ray. There is flattening of
this edge in hip dysplasia.

Dorsal Acetabular Edge This is the rim of the acetabulum, i.e. the
upper rim of the socket of the joint. In hip dysplasia, there may be
bone formation along the edge of the acetabulum, and the amount of
new bone formed along the dorsal acetabular edge is the basis for
assessment under this parameter.

Cranial Effective Acetabular Rim The cranial effective acetabular rim is formed where the cranial acetabular edge and the dorsal acetabular edge meet to form a definite point. In hip dysplasia, this point may be rounded off and, if arthritis develops, new bone formation at this site will occur.

Acetabular Fossa The head of the femur is attached to the acetabulum by a ligament and this ligament attaches to the acetabulum in the area of the acetabular fossa. Although this fossa can be seen in hip X-rays, with hip dysplasia there is new bone formation so that the fossa is more difficult to visualize.

Caudal Acetabular Edge The caudal acetabular edge is the caudal equivalent of the cranial effective acetabular rim, so called because it is nearer to the rear of the dog. In hip dysplasia new bone formation may occur at this site.

Femoral Head/Neck Exostosis The femoral head is the ball of the ball-and-socket joint and is rounded, fitting neatly into the acetabulum. In hip dysplasia, new bone formation may form around the femoral neck, which attaches the head to the body of the femur, so thickening the neck and distorting its shape.

Femoral Head Recontouring In hip dysplasia, due to the slackness in the joint, there is abnormal wear and tear resulting in recontouring (reshaping) of the head of the femur.

Each feature is scored out of 6 for each hip, except for caudal acetabular edge which is scored out of 5. This means that scores can vary from 0 to 106.

Results are forwarded to the geneticist Dr M. B. Willis. Dr Willis produces results based on the testing at regular intervals. To date, 7851 Golden Retrievers have been scored; the mean score is 18:82 and the range of scores 0 to 104. In addition, progeny-testing data is available for dogs with sufficient scored offspring. This is invaluable as it allows one to see which dogs are producing low hip-scores, which are producing high hip-scores and which dogs are improving hip-scores in relation to the score of the bitches. Three hip X-rays have been reproduced to show the changes which occur in hips with different scores. Dogs with hip-scores of 0:0 (page 182), 8:10 and 30:30 (page 183) illustrate respectively a perfect score, the average score for the Golden Retriever and a high score. The difference in the neatness of fit of the femoral head into the acetabulum is obvious in these three cases.

With the BVA/KC Hip Dysplasia Scheme, the means to improve hip status within the breed is available, but it requires the full support of everyone. It is true that hip dysplasia is only one factor to be considered in a breeding programme but at the very least, all breeding stock should have hips X-rayed and scored. The information should be used positively: breed from stock with good hips, use a dog with good hips, and preferably one who is producing offspring with good hips. Improvement may well be slow but can be achieved if the will to succeed is there. All plates should be submitted for proper assessment and scoring. On more than one occasion, owners have been told not to submit plates as the hips were bad, only to do so and be delighted to receive a low hip-score!

One final point I should like to make is be sensible over hip-scores, try not to develop a neurosis over the difference in a hip-score between, for example, 12 and 14 or 2 and 3. It is the general range which is of significance – the difference between 12 and 14 is not important, the difference between 5 and 50 is significant.

11

Some Notable Kennels of the Present Day

There are many kennels today which will be part of Golden Retriever history. They have distinguished themselves on the bench or in the field. The sphere in which they have distinguished themselves is immaterial; what matters is the achievement of excellence.

I originally intended to write this chapter about individual dogs, but limited space would necessitate my having to leave out many who should be represented. It seemed fairer to invite breeders who

The first family at Camrose. Left to right: Camrose Antony (2 CCs); Ch. Camrose Anthea; Camrose Christina (2 CCs); Ch. Camrose Fantango; Golden Camrose Tess (1 CC); and, sitting, Ch. Camrose Tantara.

The first Camrose litter (1948) by Ch. Colin of Rosecott, ex Golden
Camrose Tess. Ch. Camrose Anthea is second from the right.
(Photo Cummant)

had produced two or more champions to send me details of their achievements.

Mrs Joan Tudor's now world-famous Camrose kennel was founded with a bitch born in October 1946 and purchased from an advertisement in a local newspaper for eight guineas. This bitch was Golden Camrose Tess. It is interesting to note that other puppies were advertised for almost twice the price in the same paper but Tess was considered to be dear enough!

She turned out to be a great bargain as she produced two champions, another CC winner and a FT winner! Tess also won one CC and one Reserve CC herself. Out of a litter-sister to Ch. Dorcas Glorious of Slat, her sire was a son of Stubbings Golden Dandylyon.

Tess made her debut at Richmond Championship Show in 1947 where she was placed third under Dr Acton. One show led to another and Tess won a great deal before she was mated. All Golden Retrievers of Camrose breeding are descended from her through two of her sons: Camrose Antony (2 CCs) and Ch. Camrose Fantango, who have both had a great influence on the breed.

Ch. Camrose Fantango was the sire of Ch. Camrose Tallyrand of

Anbria, who, in his turn, sired Ch. Camrose Cabus Christopher and Ch. Davern Figaro (both very influential in the breed today). Also, when Ch. Camrose Fantango was mated to Ch. Camrose Tantara (a daughter of Camrose Antony), they produced Ch. Camrose Jessica, the dam of Ch. Camrose Nicolas of Westley from whom are descended all the present-day Styal and Westley Golden Retrievers.

Camrose Antony, who was one of Mrs Tudor's favourites, started an unbroken line of seven generations of title-holders through his daughter Ch. Camrose Tantara, when mated to one of Ch. Camrose Fantango's sons.

The Camrose Golden Retrievers have been consistently line-bred very closely to these early beginnings but the time came when an improvement in hind-quarters was needed and Christopher was bought from Mrs Zilpha Morgan (then Moriarty). He was from an outcross bitch line but sired by Tallyrand. His Cabus and Boltby lines provided exactly what Mrs Tudor wanted. Since then, the outcross Christopher line has been used to breed back into the original Camrose bitch line. All present-day Camrose Golden Retrievers combine these lines.

For several years, the dogs were owned in partnership with Miss

The famous Ch. Camrose Cabus Christopher, who was for many years the breed record-holder. (Photo Cooke)

R. Wilcock and, during that period, Mrs Tudor and Miss Wilcock bred or owned jointly for a time Ch. Camrose Fabius Tarquin, winner of twenty CCs; Ch. Styal Stephanie of Camrose, winner of twenty-seven CCs and a record-holder; Ch. Stenbury Sea Tristran of Camrose; Sh.Ch. Gyrima Wystonia of Camrose; Sh.Ch. Camrose Hardanger Fjord of Beldonburn; Ch. Camrose Waterlyric of Beldonburn and Sh.Ch. Camrose Frangipani of Beldonburn.

At the time of writing, a new Camrose title-holder has emerged: Sh.Ch. Camrose Tulfes Intirol (by Ch. Styal Scott of Glengilde, ex Sh.Ch. Gyrima Wystonia of Camrose).

Mrs Sawtell's Of Yeo kennel was founded in 1938 with a Golden Retriever puppy given to her by her husband on returning from honeymoon. The litter was very well bred, being by Dual Ch. Anningsley Stingo, ex Anningsley Dawn. This puppy, Princess of Slat, grew up to be very good-looking and was gun-trained by Mr Venables-Kyrke. She was shown at Taunton Championship Show where she won the Puppy and Junior classes, and received the following critique, written by Mr East, which appeared in *Our Dogs*: 'Good colour, sensible head, well-coupled body and a sound mover'. Mrs Sawtell has kept these four characteristics as yardsticks when breeding.

Ch. Camrose Fabius Tarquin at 6 years old. (Photo Pearce)

Ch. Masterpiece of Yeo.

It is interesting to learn that other kennels represented at that show were Torrdale, with Ch. Torrdale Betty, who won the bitch CC; and Woolley, with Ch. Lance of Woolley, who gained the dog CC. Other famous affixes of that time were Yelme, Stubbings, Dorcas and Abbott's Trust.

In 1942, Princess of Slat was mated to Ch. Anningsley Fox. A puppy was kept from the resulting litter and he eventually became Ch. Masterpiece of Yeo. He, like his parents, was gun-trained. When shows began again after the war, this dog was shown with considerable success and was used at stud.

A puppy was taken in lieu of a stud fee from a well-bred bitch called Sandy Girl. This puppy was sold at nine months old to Mrs Atkinson (née Watson), and eventually became FTCh. Musicmaker of Yeo. This dog is believed to be behind all Mrs Atkinson's famous Holway Golden Retrievers. Later, Mrs Atkinson bought Flush of Yeo from Mrs Sawtell and this puppy became FTCh. Holway Flush of Yeo (by FTCh. Mazurka of Wynford, ex Picture of Yeo).

Gold Dust of Yeo (sister to Ch. Masterpiece), was bred from, and Fame of Yeo was one of the resulting puppies. She was trained and

191

handled by Mr Venables-Kyrke in field trials, as were several other Yeo Golden Retrievers at this time. After the war, Mrs Sawtell started to train and handle her own dogs. She achieved much success and gained twenty awards in the field. There were no gundog tests then, only serious trials, but as the tests became more popular, Mrs Sawtell became interested in that more relaxed atmosphere and found them excellent for the dogs and socially enjoyable. This is an interest she retains to this day.

From Fame and Masterpiece, more Golden Retrievers were bred and shown. Later, the opportunity arose for Mrs Sawtell to buy a two-year-old bitch of mainly Torrdale breeding. She became Sh.Ch. Pandown Poppet of Yeo, and when mated to Ch. Alresford Advertiser, she produced Ringmaster of Yeo, who sired six champions.

The original working line, which traced back to Masterpiece, was retained but continued with progeny from Poppet to produce the following title-holders: Ch. Toddy Tavern Kummel of Yeo; Eng. and US Ch. Figaro of Yeo; Ch. Glennessa Amber Amanda; Ch. Contoul Robert; Ch. Battantropie Rissa and Ch. Jenny of Aldercarr.

While judging in Ireland, Mrs Sawtell admired Ch. Mandingo

Ch. and Am. Ch. Figaro of Yeo.

Ch. Deerflite Endeavour of Yeo.

Buidhe Column and booked two dog puppies out of a litter which Mandingo Marianne had at that time by Alresford Nice Fella. Marianne was out of a Ringmaster bitch called Lucky Charm of Yeo. One of these puppies was Mandingo Beau Geste of Yeo. Mrs Harkness suggested that she and Mrs Sawtell should own Mandingo Buidhe Column in partnership until he gained his title. He already had his Working Certificate in Ireland, where he was trained and handled by Jim Cranston, and Mrs Sawtell readily gained another Working Certificate in England. He soon won eight CCs and four Reserve CCs to become an English and Irish Champion. He won Best of Breed at Cruft's in 1969 when Mrs Richard Thompson judged and Her Majesty The Queen visited the Show and the Golden Retriever ring in particular.

Beau Geste won two Reserve CCs and was the sire of Ch. Deerflite Endeavour of Yeo and Ch. Deerflite Paragon, also of Ch. Royal Pal of Catcombe and several champions abroad.

From Endeavour came Ch. Concord of Yeo, by Ch. Stolford Happy Lad. This was an excellent litter as it also produced Nor. Ch. Caliph of Yeo owned by Mrs Braunerhjelm; Swed. Ch. Enterprise of Yeo owned by Stefan Jakobsson and Mrs Grete-Sofie Mjaerum's Ch. Likely Lad of Yeo. This breeding lies behind many Scandinavian dogs today.

Two puppies went to America and one to Canada. Caprice of Yeo stayed here and is the dam of Ch. Moorquest Mugwump. Mrs Sawtell retained Caravelle of Yeo who produced Ch. Challenger of Yeo Glengilde for Mr and Mrs Scholes. Caravelle of Yeo was mated to Ch. Glenavis Garry and her daughter, Carousel, went to Mrs Stonex in New Zealand where she did very well and produced many winning progeny.

Lively Lady of Yeo (by Int. Ch. Mandingo Buidhe Column, ex Ch. Jenny of Aldercarr) was mated to Pennard Golden Rudolfo and produced Yeo Christmas Rose. This line produced sound hips and good workers.

After Record of Yeo's death, Mrs Sawtell bought several of his puppies. One is Revised Edition of Yeo whom Mrs Sawtell describes

Fashion of Yeo – a field-trial winner.

194

as being a pleasure to own, having good looks, a loving personality, possessing good hips and being a competent worker.

In the mid 1950s, Mrs Sawtell owned Holway Klarinet of Yeo. She was sold and this was a move Mrs Sawtell regretted. She acknowledges that she learned 'the hard way'.

The Yeo kennel has also been very successful with English Setters. Mrs Sawtell derives great pleasure from the knowledge that her breeding lies behind many top-winning dogs of the present day, a result of planning and thought going back over half a century.

The first Golden Retriever that Mrs Morgan (then Moriarty) of the Cabus kennels had ever seen was a dog puppy given to her in 1954. He was a pet puppy, bred by Mr Leonard, and a grandson of Ch. Beauchasse Dominie.

Mrs Morgan decided she would like to try the world of dog showing and, in 1956, purchased a dog puppy from WD ('Davie') Barwise. This puppy was Beauchasse Jason (by Solway Laddie, ex Beauchasse Imprint), and was to have a considerable influence on the breed. Jason won one CC, three Reserve CCs and a Reserve Green Star. Three days after winning his CC, he caught a stone thrown by some boys which broke an incisor. He was retired from the ring at the early age of five years which was a great disappointment for his owner.

Cadet (by Beauchasse Jason, ex Brecklands Tamaris), was purchased. He was a top winner and a most influential sire. He gained his English and Irish titles, and sired six English title-holders. He won the Alison Nairn Stud Dog Progeny Cup in 1965 and 1966, and was runner-up in 1967.

In 1963 a son of Cadet, Cabus Boltby Combine (ex Sh.Ch. Boltby Sugar Bush), came to live with Mrs Morgan. He also won his English and Irish titles and went Reserve Best in Show at the Irish Kennel Club's Championship Show. He sired six title-holders and won the Stud Dog Progeny Cup in 1968, 1969, 1970 and 1971.

The next dog to join the Cabus show team was Janville Defender, out of a Show Champion bitch, Janville Renown. He gained his title and sired Ch. Camrose Matilda and the good dual-purpose Ch. Jescott Galahad. Later, Combine's sister Cabus Boltby Charmer joined the others at Cabus and made Golden Retriever history when mated to Ch. Camrose Tallyrand of Anbria. In the resulting litter, she produced Ch. Hughenden Cabus Columba (owned by Mrs Lucy Bacon), and also Ch. Cabus Caruso who in turn sired Sh.Ch. Nortonwood Canella.

This mating of Tallyrand and Charmer was repeated and from this came the legendary Ch. Camrose Cabus Christopher. He was extensively campaigned by Mrs Tudor and won forty-one CCs (making him the breed's record-holder for several years). His prowess as a sire was remarkable and resulted in twenty-seven title-holders. He won the prestigious Contest of Champion of Champions.

The Cabus dogs were truly dual-purpose: they picked up regularly during the shooting season. Few litters were bred as Mrs Morgan preferred the males. She greatly regrets not being able to keep her favourite breed at the present time.

The Melfricka kennel is owned by Fred and Meriel Hathaway. In late 1972, they lost a much-loved Collie at the age of sixteen. A Golden Retriever, Lindys Valentine, was purchased to help fill the void. An interest in showing led to the acquisition of two bitches from the Lindys kennel, Henrietta and Hermione, followed in 1975 by Lindys Butterscotch. In 1977, he gained his first CC and in 1980 became Sh.Ch. Lindys Butterscotch of Melfricka.

In 1982, Melfricka Echo (by Sh.Ch. Lindys Butterscotch of

Melfricka Xmas Wishes.

Honey of Whalley.

Melfricka, ex Lindys Violetta) became the first home-bred title-holder for this kennel. A Butterscotch son, Melfricka Frolic, then gained one CC and two Reserve CCs; his daughter Facsimile gained two CCs and two Reserve CCs.

In 1984, Melfricka Jocasta (by Ch. Camrose Cabus Christopher, ex Sh.Ch. Melfricka Echo), was awarded a CC. Her daughter Melfricka Nota Bene, by Butterscotch, gained two Reserve CCs and also Reserve Best in Show at the Golden Retriever Club of Scotland's Championship Show and Reserve Best in Show at Open Shows. Jocasta's son by Ch. Styal Scott of Glengilde became Sh.Ch. Melfricka Zed in 1987.

Sh.Ch. Melfricka Kudos of Rossbourne (owned by Mrs Burnett) sired Melfricka Xmas Wishes, who is the sire of two English champions and one Canadian champion, and is the brother of Can. Ch. Melfricka Xmas Tidings.

Melfricka Ace in the Hole (by Ch. Camrose Fabius Tarquin, ex

Sh.Ch. Melfricka Echo) has one CC and one Reserve CC. Melfricka Love Story (by Melfricka Xmas Wishes, ex Melfricka Thanksgiving) has recently completed her title.

In 1952, Mrs Rowe founded the Raynesgold kennel with a puppy from Sh.Ch. Sonnet (bred by Liz Borrow of Deerflite fame), and Wyckwold Golden Bunty. This puppy was Honey of Whalley. When Mrs Borrow saw her again at six months old, she promptly entered her for the Birmingham Championship Show, under Mrs Stonex. She won second and this started Mrs Rowe's interest in showing. This bitch won well, including gaining a CC under McDonald Daly at the Northern Golden Retriever Association Show in 1958, but was poisoned soon afterwards.

In 1961, Mrs Rowe accompanied Mrs Iles (Glennessa), to collect a dog puppy from Cheltenham and ended up bringing back a bitch puppy for herself. Mrs Rowe stated that 'Muriel Iles always said I paid too little for her!' This puppy was Raynesgold Glennessa Etoile and, when mated to Ch. Cabus Cadet in 1965, she produced a good litter containing the winners: Raynesgold Rainorshine; Raynesgold Rainaway and Raynesgold Rainabout.

In 1967, a repeat mating resulted in Sh.Ch. Raynesgold Rifleman,

Sh.Ch. Raynesgold Rifleman and Raynesgold Repose as 'Bisto Kids'!

198

Sh.Ch. Raynesgold Rifleman. (Photo Young)

Raynesgold Repose and Raynesgold Ready Response. A further repeat a year later produced Raynesgold Rochester and Raynesgold Rita.

In 1971, Raynesgold Response produced a promising puppy who eventually became Sh.Ch. Raynesgold Renown. When in 1974, she was mated to Ch. Deerflite Paragon, she produced Raynesgold Right Royal, who is the sire of Sh.Ch. Zach of Dunblair.

The Mandingo kennel is owned by Eva Harkness who, in 1955, bought her first Golden Retriever, Alexander the Great, who was a grandson of Ch. Alexander of Elsiville. Around this time, a bitch was purchased from Lucy Ross called Buidhe Dart. She was sired by Dual Ch. and Irish Ch. David of Westley.

From these two, Mrs Harkness bred two litters but having a young family she felt unable to campaign any of them at that time. Later, however, when the children began to grow up, a dog puppy, Alresford Nice Fella, was acquired from Lottie Pilkington. He won a great deal, gaining all his points for his Irish title. However, at that time, there was no such title as Show Champion in Ireland, so he remained uncrowned. He was a great showman and did much to improve the breed in Ireland.

Sh.Ch. Raynesgold Renown. (Photo Cook)

When Fella was mated to Lucky Charm of Yeo (bought from Mrs Sawtell), they produced five Irish champions, namely: Mandingo Marianne; Mandingo Marigold, Mandingo Beau Ideal; Mandingo Beau Legionnaire and Mandingo Salome. Also in this notable litter was Mandingo Beau Geste, who is to be found behind many champions.

Marigold won two CCs before she died quite young of a heart attack. She has a place in history as the dam of Ch. and Nor. Ch. Glenavis Barman, owned by Mrs Avis and later exported to Mrs Braunerhjelm of the famous Sandemars kennel in Sweden. Marianne had four Reserve CCs, and her brother Beau Ideal was a very good worker having several field-trial awards in Ireland. As well as being a champion in Ireland, he had one CC in England. Beau Legionnaire was a champion in Ireland and had three CCs and one Reserve CC in England, so gaining his English Show Champion title.

Fella also sired two further Irish Champions when mated to Miss Ross's Buidhe Dearg. These were Ch. and Irish Ch. Mandingo Buidhe Column and Irish Ch. Buidhe Curragh. Column won seven CCs and was Best of Breed at Cruft's in 1969.

Ir. Ch. Mandingo Beau Ideal.

*Eva Harkness with Ch. and Ir. Ch. Mandingo Buidhe
Column and Ir. Ch. Mandingo Marianne. (Photo Ross)*

It was unfortunate that Lucky Charm of Yeo, though a beautiful bitch could never be shown, as her leg was shattered in an accident. She was, however, an invaluable brood bitch. From Lucky and Fella, Mrs Harkness kept Mandingo Marianne, who was successful in the show ring and won her first CC when very young from the Junior class under Mrs Stonex. She also won two Gundog Groups in Ireland. She was eventually mated to Irish Ch. Bryanstown Gale Warning, which produced two more Irish champions in Mandingo Aquarious and Mandingo Angela and both had field-trial awards.

A second mating of Lucky, this time to Greenglen Country Style, produced Can. Ch. Mandingo Torrero and Dan. Ch. Mandingo Tijuana. After this mating, there was little activity by way of breeding or showing at Mandingo as several dogs were growing old and Mrs Harkness felt unable to commit herself further at that time.

In 1978, Bandmaster of Yeo was bought from Mrs Sawtell. He was a descendant of Beau Geste and Column. Later, Muskan Mink, another descendant of these two dogs was bought as a mate for Bandmaster. Bandmaster and Mink produced Irish Ch. Mandingo Playboy at Avoncraig and Mandingo Posy at Ruadth, both excellent workers and working-test winners. Mink, mated to Irish Ch. Westley Silas of Greenglen, produced Mandingo Last Love, a CACIB winner in Germany, and Mandingo Last Bet, who has Reserve Green Stars.

In 1981, Mandingo Jolly Girl was born. She is by Bandmaster out of a Greenglen bitch by Faunus. She has all the points required to be an Irish Champion but still needs her gundog qualifier to hold her title. She has produced a Junior Warrant winner in Mandingo Yours Truly, who is also a working-test winner.

The Mandingo kennel now comprises Bandmaster, Mink, Jolly Girl, Fandango Lady from Mandingo, and two new puppies of Yeo and Linchael breeding.

The Westley kennel came into being when Joan Gill acquired Simon of Brookshill as a birthday present in 1936. All present-day Westleys are descended from him through his daughter Westley Frolic of Yelme. Simon was a good Golden Retriever, but grew too tall, so Speedwell Dulcet was purchased from Mrs Evers-Swindell.

Dulcet produced a litter by Weyland Viking and the puppy who went to Jean Train (now Lumsden), was the beginning of the Treunair kennel. Dulcet and Simon should have been mated but the outbreak of war interrupted any plans of breeding, so this never materialized.

Miss Gill then bought Susan of Westley. This bitch was shown and worked and Miss Gill admits she cannot decide which was more exciting, winning Susan's first CC or her first field-trial award. Susan's second CC was at Cruft's, when she also won the Gold Trophy. This was the first Cruft's after the war and was held in October. Six Reserve CCs later, Susan won the all-important third CC.

Susan started the Westley bitch line and, mated to Spar of Yelme, produced Ch. William of Westley; mated to Dorcas Glorious of Slat, she produced Eng. and Irish Dual Ch. David of Westley, the only International dual champion in the breed and possibly in any gundog breed. Miss Gill retained David's sister Drusilla.

Lively of Yelme was mated to Simon, and Miss Gill bought Westley Frolic of Yelme. Mated to Dorcas Timberscombe Topper, she produced Ch. Sally of Westley and Ch. Willow of Westley. In her second litter, by Ch. Camrose Fantango, she produced Ch. Simon of Westley and through this dog all the Westley's go back to Simon of Brookshill.

Drusilla won a field-trial award and was mated to Ch. Simon of Westley. He won his Junior Warrant, twenty-one CCs, a Gundog Group and the Cruft's Gold Trophy five times. He won field-trial awards including a first and was the sire of CC and field-trial winners.

Echo of Westley was the result of the Simon and Drusilla mating. She won seventeen field-trial awards and produced a champion and a field-trial champion. Ch. William was mated to Ch. Camrose Jessica when he was almost eleven years old. Sadly, he died when the puppies were only a few weeks old. Ch. Camrose Nicolas of Westley was from this litter. He won twenty CCs, Junior Warrant, three field-trial awards, three Gundog Groups, Best in Show and Reserve Best in Show at Championship Shows and the Cruft's Gold Trophy three times. He won the Stud Dog Cup and sired six champions and six field-trial winners.

A move to Oxfordshire came next and Echo had a litter by FTCh. Holway Lancer. Their son, FTCh. Holway Teal of Westley was second in the Retriever Championship. From her next litter by Nicolas, she produced Ch. Pippa of Westley. Pippa won seventeen CCs and, for ten years, held the record for most CCs won by a bitch. She was the best dual-purpose Golden Retriever in 1970 and also won two field-trial awards and the Cruft's Golden Trophy. Her first litter was by Daniel of Westley (son of Ch. Simon), who died at only five and a half years of age. Samantha was retained and the present champion-bitch line traces to her.

Ch. Pippa's litter by Ch. Sansue Camrose Phoenix produced Australian Ch. Calrossie of Westley. Daphne Philpott had Clarissa of Westley from this litter. It was when Mrs Philpott generously allowed Joan Gill to share a litter from Clarissa that the partnership of Gill and Philpott began.

Samantha's second litter to Ch. Crouchers Leo produced Ch. Westley Jacquetta, who won seven CCs and the Cruft's Gold Trophy twice. Clarissa won eight CCs and Ch. Sansue Saracen of Westley was also made up. In 1973 Jacquetta was mated to Ch. Sansue Camrose Phoenix and from the resulting four puppies, the only bitch in the litter was kept. She became Ch. Westley Victoria, whose influence in the breed is enormous. She was given to Mervyn Philpott.

Victoria is the top-producing bitch of all time having produced eight English title-holders, and also an American, Canadian and Irish

A son of Aust. Ch. Calrossie of Westley, American Ch. Nordlys Australis, the first Australian-bred Golden Retriever to become an American champion.

An impressive line of Westley champions. Left to right: Sh.Ch. Westley Simone, Ch. Westley Topic of Sansue, Ch. Westley Victoria, Ch. Westley Mabella, and Ch. Westley Martha. (Photo Dalton)

champion. She won the Golden Retriever Club's bitch progeny cup three times. Her title-holders are Ch. Westley Topic of Sansue, Sh.Ch. Westley Tartan of Buidhe, Sh.Ch. Westley Simone, Sh.Ch. Westley Sophia of Papeta, Ch. Westley Samuel, Ch. Westley Mabella, Ch. Westley Martha, and Sh.Ch. Westley Munro of Nortonwood.

Mervyn Philpott, Daphne's husband, took out a separate interest in the affix and to make it more complicated, Daphne and Joan have a joint interest in the Standerwick affix, which Daphne uses for her English Setters. It was decided to use it for the field-trial bred Golden Retrievers, starting with Strathcarron Seil of Standerwick, winner of two field-trial awards.

From the mating of Ch. Victoria to Ch. Nortonwood Faunus, Joan and Daphne kept Martha and Mervyn chose Mabella. Both became champions, Mabella winning twenty CCs and a Group, and Martha winning five CCs. Mabella's progeny include Ch. Westley Felicia of Siatham, Sh.Ch. Westley Jacob, and Westley Julianna with one CC. Martha produced Ch. Westley Ramona.

Samuel, as well as being a top winner, is an accepted hip-improver.

He is the sire of Ch. Sansue Xtra Polite. Ch. Westley Jacob won six CCs and two Gundog Groups. The most recent winner was Westley Christina, who won her first CC at Darlington and also the Group.

There have been twenty-five Westley title-holders and one International dual champion.

The Standerwick kennel was started by Daphne Philpott, who worked Ch. Westley Jacquetta and became interested in Golden Retrievers of field-trial breeding. Strathcarron Seil of Standerwick was purchased from Mrs Macrae. She was mated to FTCh. Holway Spinner, which produced Ch. Standerwick Thomasina, who was Best Dual-Purpose Golden Retriever in 1984. Seil is the dam of FTCh. Standerwick Roberta of Abnalls and FTCh. Standerwick Rumbustious of Catcombe and grandam of FTCh. Standerwick Donna of Deadcraft.

Roberta won fourth in the 1986 Championship. Daphne bought Roberta's daughter by Holway Drummer; Abnalls Evita of Standerwick. She won the Golden Retriever Club's Open Stake in 1987 and also won a Diploma of Merit at the Retriever Championship at Sandringham the same year. Abnalls Hilary of Standerwick is the most recent field-trial champion.

Strathcarron Seil of Standerwick aged 13.

Seil with daughters FTCh. Standerwick Roberta of Abnalls and Ch.
Standerwick Thomasina. (photo Sally Anne Thompson)

The first Standerwick litter was bred in 1979 and, up to the present time, twenty-two Standerwicks have gained trial awards.

Mr and Mrs Lowe of the Davern kennel have owned or bred eight English title-holders. Their interest in the breed started in 1963 when Sutton Rudy arrived. He was the last of the litter and had not been chosen before because he was dark! He eventually became Ch. Sutton Rudy and won field-trial awards.

The next puppy was Camrose Flavella (by Ch. Camrose Nicolas of Westley, ex Camrose Wistansy). Camrose Wistansy was much admired and when she was mated to Int. Ch. Cabus Cadet, Camrose Pruella was purchased. She gained her title and was Best in Show at the Three Counties Championship Show in 1969. All the Davern Golden Retrievers are descended from these three bitches and carry their lovely temperaments.

Pruella was mated to Ch. Camrose Tallyrand of Anbria, and Ch. Davern Figaro was the result, as was Swed. Ch. Davern Fergus. Figaro sired Ch. Pinecrest Salvador, Ch. Deremar Dinah, Sh.Ch. Nortonwood Checkmate, Sh.Ch. Camrose Frangipani of Beldon-burn, and Sh.Ch. Davern Josephine. Josephine, owned by Mrs Beck,

FTCh. Abnalls Hilary of Standerwick. (photo Sally Anne Thompson)

Ch. Camrose Pruella of Davern. (Photo Pearce)

won eighteen CCs and was one of the top winning bitches. Figaro was mated to Davern Gabriella (by Ch. Camrose Cabus Christopher, ex Davern Astella) producing Josephine; Joyella, with one CC, who sadly died in whelp at three years old; and Jollyfella (four Reserve CCs). When Jollyfella was mated to Davern Fenella (Figaro's sister), this produced Sh.Ch. Davern Rosabella, who was then mated to Ch. Lacons Enterprise to produce Sh.Ch. Davern Alpine Rose.

It was felt that an outcross was needed and the next two champions were bought in for this purpose, namely: Sh.Ch. Verdayne Dandini (by Ch. Brensham Audacity, ex Verdayne Charlotte), and Sh.Ch. Amirene King Eider of Davern (by Sh.Ch. Nortonwood Checkmate, ex Stalyhills Miss Avenger of Amirene). Both were Figaro grandsons. Ch. Davern Figaro is behind two famous Scandinavian dogs: Nor. Ch. Lion Lotchek (top stud-dog in Norway in 1979 and 1980); and also Swed. Ch. Deremar Donald (top stud-dog in Sweden in 1979).

Another Davern dog to produce CC winners and other top-winning Golden Retrievers is Camrose Fidelio of Davern (by Ch. Davern Figaro, ex Sh.Ch. Gyrima Wystonia of Camrose).

The Davern kennel stresses that as well as show dogs, all their Golden Retrievers are much-loved pets. It has never been their intention to break records but to enjoy showing and working the dogs and to produce sound, typical Golden Retrievers who carry all the characteristics that make the breed so remarkable.

The Garbank prefix is derived from the name of the Crosbies' first home, 'Grongarbank'. Gladys Crosbie obtained her first Golden Retriever from Margaret and Fred Triptree. He was Knight of Brambletyne.

Jasmine of Dowally, the foundation bitch for this kennel arrived at nine months old. It is worth recounting the strange events of this bitch's entry into the world. Her dam Sheba disappeared into the Perthshire hills just before she was due to whelp. Eventually, a very thin Sheba arrived at her owners' door. They followed her and two miles away they discovered her puppies, nine of them, under the roots of a tree.

Jasmine was mated but entropion appeared in the litter, as did bad mouths. She was eventually mated again, this time to Ch. Greenwards Latin Boy of Kirkton. The one bitch in the litter was retained and she became Sh.Ch. Garbank Charming Cindy.

When Cindy was a puppy, she was shown at the last Scottish

Kennel Club Championship Show to be held in the Kelvin Hall in Glasgow in 1974. Cindy won Best Puppy and Jasmine won the Reserve CC. Cindy won well, including Best in Show at Open Shows. She won her three CCs by the end of 1977 and was the first Scottish owned and bred title-holder in the breed. When Cindy was mated to Ch. Brierford Briar of Bessram, Garbank Wildfowl (Reserve CC) and Garbank Winsome Lass were the result. Winsome Lass's daughter, Garbank Golden Oriole, is the dam of Ch. Bethrob Bracken. Another highly successful mating to Ch. Camrose Fabius Tarquin produced Ch. and Irish Ch. Garbank Special Edition of Lislone.

Braydan Classic of Garbank joined the kennel and won her Junior Warrant, and by the time she was three and a half years old, she had won four CCs. She reappeared in the ring three years later where she won the CC and Best of Breed.

Bracken is the Garbank who carries his full title and was almost four years old before his owner, Jim Crosbie, started to train him. Within three months, he gained his qualifying certificate at a field trial in Scotland. Bracken has puppies in Scandinavia, conceived from frozen semen. Half the semen has been used and one bitch from the litter this produced is owned by the vet who collected the semen.

June Atkinson founded the Holway kennel with a Golden Retriever in 1947. This was Musicmaker of Yeo (by Ch. Masterpiece of Yeo). Mrs Atkinson was a spectator at the Retriever Championship at Hungerford and set her standard on the work she saw there.

Music was trained almost entirely on rabbits, going out shooting each evening with the keeper's son. The first trial was the United Gundog Breeders Novice in Shropshire, which Music won. Next came the Scottish Golden Retriever Trials and Music won two Open Stakes making her a field-trial champion. Whilst there, Mrs Atkinson met the Frazers (of Westhyde) and Music was later mated to the young Westhyde Stubblesdown Major (later to become a field-trial champion) and this mating produced Mazurka of Wynford.

Mazurka was a truly great dog winning the Retriever Championship in 1954. His son Holway Zest became the next field-trial champion. Mr Martin Atkinson handled Zest to second in the Championship. The next Holways were Lancer and Bonnie, both out of Melodymaker, Mazurka's sister.

Holway Westhyde Zeus (Zest's son) was the next field-trial champion for this kennel. He sired Holway Barrister and Holway

Jollity. These two, and Gaiety, were all out of FTCh. Holway Flush of Yeo, Mazurka's daughter.

FTCh. Holway Chanter was the kennel's next title-holder and he was by Palgrave Enchanter. Chanter sired Little Marston Chorus of Holway, who won the Retriever Championship in 1982 at Sandringham, handled by Mrs Atkinson's son Robert. Holway Gem (out of Gaiety) produced Dollar, Ruby and Grettle, the latter two being by Riot, an excellent worker who was unlucky not to gain his title. Jollity was a family favourite, winning a Novice Stake with Robert, an Open Stake with daughter Jane, and further awards with Mrs Atkinson. Chorus has produced two field-trial champions in Trumpet and Corbiere.

Mrs Atkinson would find it an impossible task to nominate her 'best' dog. Gaiety, Chanter, Chorus and Ruby have all won the Routledge-Rank Cup awarded to the retriever of any breed winning most points at field trials during the season.

Two of this kennel's great triumphs occurred when Mazurka won

FTCh. Mazurka of Wynford delivering his last bird to hand on his way to winning the Retriever Championships in 1954.

Six of Mrs Atkinson's field-trial champions, 1987. Left to right:
Holway Chorus, Gem, Dollar, Grettle, Chanter, and Trumpet.

the Retriever Championship in 1954, and Chorus, Mazurka's great, great, great grand-daughter, handled by Robert, won the same event in 1982.

My own kennel, Linchael, began in 1965 with the acquisition of two dog puppies, which was not the most sensible way to start a kennel. These were Myrtlehill Magnificent, (by Ch. Camrose Tallyrand of Anbria, ex Irish Ch. Weeton Witch of Ouzeldale) bred by Stewart in Ireland, and Wildwind Byron (by Camrose Anbria Fergus, ex Camrose Unity) bred by Daphne Weston.

My sole interest in the breed was obedience, but a friend persuaded me to enter for Cruft's in 1967 (there was no qualifying rule in those days) and my dogs won a first and a VHC (very highly commended) under the formidable Mrs Wentworth-Smith.

They won well at Open Shows and had the odd placing at Championship Shows but I soon realized that to make the grade I would have to look elsewhere. My first bitch puppy came from Mrs Hinks and she was Styal Seamist (by Ch. Gamebird Debonair of Teecon, ex Sh.Ch. Styal Sibella). She won some very large classes at Championship Shows but never regained her figure after her litter by Sean of Westley. The bitch puppy I retained developed entropion, so it was a case of starting again.

Three bought-in bitch puppies eventually developed cataract. On each occasion, this was diagnosed when the bitches were already Championship Show winners. Perhaps the hardest blow of all came when a top-winning young dog and one of the last of a very famous line was diagnosed as having not only cataract but also PRA (Progressive Retinal Atrophy) at eight years old. He had been examined for every year of his life. This disappointment was very hard to accept and so nearly ended my association with the breed.

Then Mrs Harrison (of Janville) gave me the chance to choose a puppy from one of several litters she had at that time. I chose a bitch, but it was not to be – she injured a leg before it was time to collect her. The only other puppy I liked was a dog, but I did not want a male. I took him home! This puppy began a successful few years for me. He became Sh.Ch. Janville Tempestuous at Linchael (by Deerflite Tradition of Janville, ex Janville Kristeen). At Open Show level, he won over fifty Best of Breed awards and was a consistent winner at Championship Shows from his very first one, Manchester, where he was awarded Best Puppy in Breed, to the time when he gained his title.

Sh.Ch. Linchael Heritage winning Best of Breed at Cruft's in 1984. The judge is Mrs Lucy Bacon (centre) and Ch. Brensham Audacity is on the right.

Sh.Ch. Linchael Excelsior.

In 1976, two bitch puppies were purchased and these were to have a great influence on the formation of my kennel. One was Deerflite Destiny and the other Rossbourne Angelene. Destiny (by Deerflite Curtana, ex Deerflite Enchanting) was one of the most beautiful bitches I had seen. She was very dark gold and positively gleamed. She had a lovely head and her shoulders and hind angulation were perfect. Unfortunately, she hated showing but was a most useful brood. Mated to Sh.Ch. Janville Tempestuous at Linchael, she produced Sh.Ch. Linchael Heritage, who was a most consistent winner. She gained a triple Junior Warrant and quickly earned her title. This successful run culminated in Best of Breed at Cruft's in 1984. Heritage was also a multiple Best in Show winner. She was not a successful brood, producing just one small, rather mediocre litter and later a litter of ten dead puppies. Later, when Destiny was mated to Ch. Bryanstown Gaucho, she produced Sh.Ch. Linchael Excelsior.

Rossbourne Angelene (by Stenbury Seawizard, ex Glennessa Omega) did like showing but she was a clown and could not resist playing to the gallery. When asked to move by the judge, she would

214

set off at a smart pace, then suddenly stop for a good scratch. On one occasion, having won a good class at a Championship Show, she had a roll on the judge's feet as he attempted to write his critique! I knew when I was beaten as far as showing was concerned, but Anna was to gain a place in Golden Retriever history through the record of her daughter.

When Anna was mated to Ch. Camrose Fabius Tarquin, I retained Linchael Delmoss and Linchael Casamayor. It was Grand National Day when they were born, so I named them after two of the runners. A second mating of Anna to Tarquin produced Sh.Ch. Linchael Freya of Gloi. Casamayor won well at Championship Shows, but never gained his title, ending his career with six Reserve CCs and one CC.

Delmoss was a most reluctant showlady but so very well constructed that I persevered. She gained her title and I never showed her again as she hated it so much. I took her to be mated to Glengilde Statesman who simply would not have anything to do with her, so she was mated to his sire Ch. Styal Scott of Glengilde instead. What a substitute he proved to be! This first mating produced Cartier,

Sh.Ch. Linchael Delmoss, one of the breed's famous brood-bitches, having produced 7 champions. Pictured with daughter Linchael Chantilly.

Cellini and Chantilly. They all gained their Junior Warrants quite quickly. Then Cartier gained his title, but my greatest thrill occurred when his hips were X-rayed and he scored 0:0. Cellini at this time has one CC and three Reserve CCs. Chantilly won very well as a junior but had a weight problem which was almost impossible to control, so her show career was prematurely terminated. Chantilly proved herself to be of value: when mated back to her grandsire Ch. Camrose Fabius Tarquin, she produced Fin Ch. Linchael Ravel.

The next mating of Delmoss to Scott produced the 'Wild' bunch. These were Fin. Ch. Linchael Wild Rose, Ch. Linchael Wild Silk, Linchael Wild Thyme (Green Star Winner), Linchael Wild Orchid (Green Star winner), and Linchael Wild Cherry.

The third time I mated Delmoss to Scott, she produced Linchael Corniche (one CC, Finland), and a good winner at Championship level: Linchael Medici. It also produced Irish Ch. Linchael Silver Ghost and Linchael Silver Spirit (two CCs, Norway).

I felt I was really pushing my luck to do this mating yet again, but I did, and Sh.Ch. Linchael Conspiracy and Nor. Ch. Linchael Conclusion were the most rewarding result.

One of my greatest disappointments was that Linchael Wild Cherry died of leukaemia when her litter was just six weeks old. She

Ir. Ch. Linchael Silver Ghost of Strathearn.

216

Breed history in the making: brother and sister, Sh.Ch. Linchael
Conspiracy of Chevanne and Ch. Linchael Wild Silk winning their
third CCs on the same day at the Welsh Kennel Club Championship
Show 1990.

lives on through her son in Sweden, Linchael Myrrh who has just won his third CC; and through Linchael Clouded Yellow (two CCs in Sweden). Perhaps the greatest thrill was when Ch. Linchael Wild Silk and Sh.Ch. Linchael Conspiracy of Chevanne both took their titles on the same day. This would be a great achievement at any time, but more so as they are brother and sister.

The future looks interesting as Mjaerumhogda's Thyra recently joined me from Norway and has a litter by Nor. Ch. Mjaerumhogda's Crusader, who has been on loan to me for two years. Thyra is unique as she is the product of mating by artificial insemination from frozen semen to the great Ch. Camrose Cabus Christopher, who has been dead for so many years. From her litter I have retained Linchael Gullviva (Swedish for 'Primrose').

One more puppy has been chosen to stay: Linchael Persian Orchid. He is from the litter out of Linchael Wild Orchid by Nor. Ch. Mjaerumhogda's Crusader. With these two I look forward to starting my next quarter-century in the ring. 1990 ended on a splendid note with the news that Delmoss had gained the much-coveted Top Brood Bitch award.

Carol Gilbert of the Okus kennel had wanted a Golden Retriever since her childhood. Her first dog was a Golden Retriever/Samoyed cross. A few years elapsed before a pure-bred Golden Retriever was acquired. This was Ellendune Gay Jessie, known as Laiki (by Ch. Westley Joshua, ex Ellendune Gay Lady), bred by Mrs Sheppard. Since she carried three well-known lines, Westley, Camrose and Stolford, she was a sound foundation.

A visit to an Exemption Show with Laiki, where she won a rosette, was the start of an interest in showing. Entries were made to a few Championship Shows, but although Laiki was well constructed she lacked in both head and coat, although the latter was to grow profusely in later life.

Mrs Gilbert then purchased a bitch puppy, who was to become Saffron Dawn of Okus, from Mrs Sheppard. She was out of a Ch. Camrose Cabus Christopher daughter by Sh.Ch. Concord of Yeo. As Mrs Sheppard was having problems registering a litter born eighteen months before, she suggested this one was registered by Carol. This explains how the puppy bears Carol's affix and not that of her breeder. Okus seemed a sound choice of affix: it was short, so allowing for more letters in the chosen name (which the Kennel Club restricts to twenty-four) and it was the name of a nearby district.

Laiki was mated to the then young Brensham Audacity (who was later to take his title and many CCs). He was much admired at Cruft's by Mrs Gilbert, who was naturally delighted when he won not only the CC and Best of Breed, but also the Group. The resulting litter included Okus Autumn Adventurer, who was to become a great family favourite. He won well, taking his Junior Warrant and winning through the classes up to and including Limit at Championship Shows. A good stud-dog, he sired Okus Impact (two Reserve CCs).

By the time Dawn was old enough to be bred from, Mrs Gilbert had already decided that Ch. Moorquest Mugwump was the most suitable dog for her. Three puppies resulted and two survived. Both were retained and these were Okus Buccaneer and Okus Bronze Brocade (who was later to produce Okus Impact).

Buccaneer was special from the moment he was on his feet. He won Best Puppy in Breed and Reserve Best Puppy in Show at his very first show at just six months old. Then the unthinkable happened. Just over a month later he was dying with the 'new' disease, parvovirus. He underwent three major operations in ten days. His intestines were both twisted and perforated. During the last operation he 'died' three times, receiving cardiac stimulation to restart his heart and three pints of blood by transfusion.

Miraculously, he was back in the ring at eleven months old, winning Best Puppy in Show at the Golden Retriever Club of Wales Championship Show. By fifteen months he had attained his Junior Warrant. At nineteen months he won his first Reserve CC and a month later he gained his Show Gundog Working Certificate. His first CC was won when he was two years and two days old. Two must have been his lucky number as exactly two months later he became the breed's youngest ever full champion.

The heart damage caused by parvovirus took its toll when he retired from public stud very early. In the short time he was used, he sired two champions, four CC winners and many other winners. One of his early litters was out of Laiki and this produced Ch. Okus Jallina of Kerrien, a bitch as happy working as she is in the show ring. She is behind all the Kerrien winners, including those who have won CCs and Reserve CCs.

Okus Qui Vive.

Sh.Ch. Okus Watersprite, top CC-winning bitch 1989.

Buccaneer was mated to Impact three times. Of all the three bitch puppies that resulted, one was Okus Qui Vive and the other Okus Songbird of Crowood (two CCs and one Reserve CC).

It was felt that the introduction of an outcross would be beneficial at this time and Papeta Phedra (by Ch. Sansue Golden Ruler, ex Westley Sophia of Papeta) was purchased. In due course, she was mated to Okus Vendric Voyager. Of the twelve puppies born, one stood out as having everything. This early impression proved accurate as, by two years and three months of age, she was Sh.Ch. Okus Watersprite and was the top CC-winning bitch of 1989.

The Okus kennel has bred nine Junior Warrant winners, two champions, one show champion, two other CC winners and a Reserve CC winner. Mrs Gilbert feels she owes much to the good training given to her by Mrs Sheppard, who set very high standards. Mrs Gilbert is quick to point out, 'It is easy to watch someone winning in the ring and think they have all the luck. Believe me, we all suffer for our success at some time and I sometimes think that the greater the success, the greater the disaster to compensate'.

The foundation bitch of the Sansue kennel was Tingel Concorde (by Daniel of Westley, ex Sh.Ch. Tingel Ripple of Arbrook), born in 1964. A sound bitch to start with, she won two Reserve CCs, produced two litters, won veteran classes at fifteen years and died just before her seventeenth birthday.

The next acquisition was a dog puppy called Camrose Phoenix, bought from Mrs Tudor in 1965. He was by Int. Ch. Cabus Cadet, ex Camrose Wistansy. He took his title, won fourteen CCs, including Best of Breed at Cruft's, and was Best in Show at the Golden Retriever Club's Championship Show in 1971. With two exceptions, all present-day Sansue's are descended from Phoenix and Concorde.

Phoenix became sterile at eight years following an operation but had a big influence on the breed, producing several champions, the most famous being Ch. Westley Victoria. In the next twelve years, the following were produced: Ch. Sansue Saracen of Westley, Sh.Ch. Milo Hollybush of Sansue, Ch. Sansue Tobias, Ch. Westley Topic of Sansue, and Ch. Sansue Cressida of Manoan. Hollybush was sired by Phoenix and all the others are out of Phoenix daughters.

In 1977, a bitch puppy was retained from the mating of Gyrima Moonlord of Rockwin to Sansue Gillian. She became Sh.Ch. Sansue Wrainbow, dam of four English champions and an International

Ch. Gaineda Consolidator of Sansue (10 CCs). Best of Breed at Cruft's in 1987.

221

champion. (Wrainbow's litter-sister, Sansue Wanda of Stirchley is the dam of Sh.Ch. Stirchley Saxon).

In 1978, Gaineda Consolidator (by Glennessa Escapade, ex Sh.Ch. Rachenco Charnez of Gaineda) joined the kennel. He won over 100 Junior Warrant points and soon became Ch. Gaineda Consolidator of Sansue, winning ten CCs. He was Best of Breed at Cruft's in 1987. He has sired nine champions, three of these being home bred from Sh.Ch. Sansue Wrainbow, namely: Ch. Sansue Pepper of Lovehayne, Sh.Ch. Sansue Phoebe and Ch. Sansue Golden Ruler. Sansue Golden Gloria has one CC. Ch. Sansue Golden Ruler has twenty-three CCs. He is a Gundog Group and a Best in Show winner. He has sired five champions and other CC winners. He is the holder of the Alison Nairn Stud-Dog trophy and has a winning brother in Scandinavia, Nordic and Swed. Ch. Sansue Golden Arrow.

The Westley Brood-Bitch Trophy is currently held by Rossbourne Party Piece of Sansue (by Ch. Westley Topic of Sansue, ex Rossbourne Breeze). Party Piece was mated to Ruler and produced three Champions: Ch. Sansue Royal Fancy, Ch. Sansue Royal Flair and Ch. Sansue Spring Mist of Ramblyne. Mated to Sh.Ch. Styal Shelley of Maundale, she produced Sansue Castalian (one CC, three Reserve CCs).

The most recent title-holder for this kennel is Ch. Sansue Xtra Polite (by Ch. Westley Samuel, ex Sh.Ch. Sansue Wrainbow). She is the dam of Can. Ch. Sansue Lochinvar and Nor. Ch. Sansue Lollipop Vivi.

Mrs Anderson began her Gaineda kennel with the acquisition of Gainspa Fanfare (Int. Ch. Cabus Boltby Combine, ex Sh.Ch. Gainspa Oonah). He won a great deal, including five CCs, each with the Best of Breed and Reserve in the Group at Cruft's in 1974. His career ended prematurely when he tore a ligament in his hind leg, which left him with an intermittent limp.

The next puppy for this kennel came from Mr R. Jacobs: Peradenia Glamour Girl. When mated to Fanfare, a dog puppy called Gaineda Pearly Baer was retained from the resulting litter. These Golden Retrievers all won well but several problems arose and it was decided to start afresh with different lines. Two puppies were purchased from Mrs Temperley, called Melling Araminta and Melling Apollinaire. The dog grew too tall and although the bitch won well, she never produced any outstanding offspring.

A bitch puppy, Rachenco Charnez, was collected from Mrs Cochrane. What an influence on the breed this bitch was to prove. A Ch.

Camrose Cabus Christopher daughter, she was to go from strength to strength. She began by winning her Junior Warrant at nine and a half months old. Very soon she won her first Reserve CC. Eventually she was mated to Glennessa Escapade. From this mating, Gaineda It's Magic was retained and Mrs Birkin bought Gaineda Consolidator. Consolidator's success is documented elsewhere but he gained his title, won numerous CCs and was a Cruft's Best of Breed winner, as was Charnez.

Mrs Warren made up Sh.Ch. Gaineda Lost Heritage of Tarnbrook (sister to It's Magic and Consolidator). This bitch caused a stir when she won her first Reserve CC at six and a half months old.

In the short time It's Magic was shown, she won most of her classes but before she was a year old cataract was diagnosed, so this brought any thoughts of breeding to a halt. Since a very promising dog bred earlier, Gaineda To Flight, had been withdrawn from the ring for the same reason, this news was devastating.

Charnez was mated to Rachenco Maestro. From this litter, Gaineda Gospel was retained for showing. When Gospel was mated to Tonara Rainbeau of Roscraddoc, Gaineda Magic Touch was the result. This bitch also produced the Junior Warrant winning bitch Gaineda Chasing Rainbows, by Ch. Sansue Golden Ruler.

Charnez was later mated to Malhamdale Jason's Fleece and Gaineda Sweet 'n' Sassy was the result. She won her Junior Warrant but lost her front teeth when she caught a stone thrown by some children. This bitch was, in turn, mated to Camrose Fidelio of Davern and this, and a repeat mating, produced Gaineda Chique-Chic (Junior Warrant) and Mrs Graham's Gaineda Ivory Silk of Deneford (one CC and two Reserve CCs), and also Mrs Henderson's Reserve CC winner, Gaineda Isabella of Rusheba.

From Chique-Chic the latest member of the Gaineda family has emerged. She is Gaineda Strawberry Blonde (by Sh.Ch. Linchael Conspiracy of Chevanne). A rich-gold bitch, she has started well by winning her first class at a Championship Show. This mating was done previously and produced Mr McKenzie's Junior-Warrant winner, Gaineda Gunnin' for Gold.

Charnez was mated to Linchael Casamayor and Gaineda Counterfeiter of Somley resulted. He was rarely shown but won a Reserve CC when Maureen Anderson handled him at a show just before he joined the author's kennel. Here he was a consistent winner in Limit and Open classes and at the present time has one CC and four Reserve CCs. He was at stud for a short time until he became sterile at seven years old. He sired Miss Sandra Birkin's Sansue Flair's Rapture who won a Reserve CC at a very early age. Charnez eventually won ten CCs and eight Reserve CCs. She was Best of Breed at Cruft's in 1978 and won two Best in Show awards.

The Gaineda kennel has produced some willing workers. Mr and Mrs Hay's Gaineda Cantaloupe of Holywear (sister to Counterfeiter), is a working-test winner. Chique-Chic, Strawberry Blonde and Gee Whizz also work well.

The Lacons kennel came into being in 1969 when Lindys Donacilla was bought from Lindy Anderson. Donna was eventually mated to Byxfield Lindys Golden Gleam and, from the resulting litter, Lacons Analiesa (Lisa) was chosen. Lisa hated the show ring but managed to win one Reserve CC. She produced four litters to Ch. Camrose Cabus Christopher. As a result of the success of her progeny, Lisa won the Westley Brood-Bitch Cup for four consecutive years. The first litter produced five puppies. A bitch who was later to become

Sh.Ch. Rachenco Charnez of Gaineda winning Best of Breed at Cruft's in 1978.

Sh.Ch. Lacons Candy Floss was retained. She won her Junior Warrant at ten months and won a total of eight CCs and seven Reserve CCs. She won Best in Show at Blackpool Championship Show in 1978. That same year she won Best in Show at the Midland Golden Retriever Club's first Championship Show, in an entry of 744. Her litter-mates included Dan. Ch. Lacons Perry and Lacons Charioteer (one CC).

Sh.Ch. Lacons Enterprise came from the second mating of Lisa and Christopher. He won his Junior Warrant at seven and a half months and later a total of ten CCs and eight Reserve CCs. He won Best of Breed at Cruft's in 1977 and was in the final four for the Group. In 1978, he was Reserve Best in Show at the United Retriever Club's Championship Show. The same year, Enterprise and Candy Floss won both CCs at Birmingham City, and Enterprise was Reserve in the Gundog Group.

Another dog of note in this litter was Singapore Ch. Lacons Edelweiss. When her owners returned to live in England she was mated to Sh.Ch. Teecon Knight Errant and this produced Sh.Ch. Pitcote Arcadian of Garthfield, who was Best of Breed at Cruft's in 1983. Candy Floss was then mated to Ch. Sansue Tobias to produce Int. and Dan. Ch. Lacons Honey Lover.

Davern Alpine Rose (by Sh.Ch. Lacons Enterprise, ex Sh.Ch. Davern Rosabella) was purchased in 1978. She won her Junior Warrant and later won five CCs and five Reserve CCs. Her major award was the CC at the Golden Retriever Club show in 1984 and Reserve in the Group at Manchester the same year.

The next Golden Retriever to join this kennel was Camrose Kaspar of Lacons. He won very well as a puppy, winning his Junior Warrant at under nine months. A few months later he sustained a severe back injury and was unshown for three years. He returned to the ring and won one CC but soon after he was affected by arthritis and was permanently retired from the ring.

The truly dual-purpose Bryanstown kennel is owned by Cynthia and Michael Twist. Both have connections with the breed from 1946, but it was not until their marriage in 1951 that the prefix was registered. However, Michael had a Golden Retriever as a gundog in 1946 and that same year, Cynthia (née Goodbody), acquired Pennard Golden David from Mrs R. Thompson's well-known kennel. In 1951, David was to become the first ever champion of the breed in Eire.

When Cynthia expressed a wish to breed Golden Retrievers, her

Cynthia Goodbody (later Mrs Twist) with Pennard Golden David (later to gain his title), Pennard Golden Drusilla and Pennard Golden Gem (David's dam). Mrs Richard Thompson with Pennard Golden Drummer.

husband agreed with the proviso that any produced were to be of the same high standard as the bloodstock and pedigree herds that he managed for the second Duke of Westminster. Cynthia readily agreed but added her own condition that however good the Golden Retrievers they produced were for work, they must be able to hold their own in the show ring. On this basis, a dual-purpose kennel was established.

The All-Ireland Golden Retriever Club was formed in 1953 by Cynthia and Michael Twist. At their first field trial held in 1954, an Open Stake, five of the nine runners were by Irish Ch. Pennard Golden David. All five were successful show dogs.

It is worthy of note, and a great achievement, that the Twists were so adamant in their resolve to have dual-purpose Golden Retrievers, that at one time their kennel included three champions who were all Open Stakes winners. These three were regularly trialled and shown.

Part of Cynthia's wedding present from Michael was a blank

cheque to enable her to buy the best bitch she could find. This resulted in Westhyde Rona (by Stubbings Golden Nicholas) coming to live at Bryanstown. The foundations of line-breeding were established as Nicholas was the sire of Pennard Golden Gem, David's dam. Both Rona and David's pedigrees went back to the famous Ch. Birling James and Gilder.

The first litter produced Titania of Bryanstown, who consistently featured in the awards at field trials and only missed her Champion title on the bench by one point.

Diplomat of Ulvin (by Ch. Weyland Varley, ex Ch. Charming of Ulvin) joined the kennel. Sadly, as the result of illness, he proved to be sterile. He was an excellent gundog and won many awards at field trials. He quickly became a champion.

The next Golden Retrievers to join the kennel were Shannon of Yeo and Camrose Gail. Both very quickly became champions, won Open Stakes and missed their dual titles by a fraction. It is from

Left to right: Bryanstown Solo, Bryanstown Seamus and Ch. and Ir. Ch. Bryanstown Gale Warning. The premier picking-up team for this kennel in 1978. (Photo Elm Studio)

these two that all current Bryanstowns are descended. The original David/Rona line was lost.

Shannon mated to Gail produced Eng. and Irish Ch. Bryanstown Gale Warning who won eleven Green Stars and eleven CCs. He was also a tremendous worker. He won numerous trials including first in an Any Variety Retriever Open Stake. He was also fourth in the Irish Retriever Championships – a most prestigious win. This is believed to be a unique award for a champion on the bench.

The kennel was reduced before the Twists moved to England in 1970. Soon after settling in England, Crouchers Nikita (by Sh.Ch. Anbria Tantalus, ex Crouchers Ina) was purchased. She was a consistent winner (including one CC), and she picked up successfully.

Bryanstown Gale Warning made his debut at the Golden Retriever Club's Championship Show in 1970. He won Open, the Field-Trial class, the Dog CC and Best in Show. A memorable occasion, as other dogs from this kennel acquitted themselves admirably. Bryanstown Shannon Gale (Gale Warning's brother) won two classes.

Ch. Bryanstown Gaucho, winner of 18 CCs. Best of Breed at Cruft's in 1981.

Over the next twenty years the kennel has had much success including the Cardiff Championship Show in 1973 where Bryanstown dogs won six firsts, both CCs and Best of Breed. This is possibly a breed record.

Bryanstown Seamus set another record. He was by FTCh. Palgrave Holway Folly, a dog of pure field-trial breeding and he sired a CC winner. Seamus won well in the ring but his title eluded him. The late Eric Baldwin, an accepted authority on field trials, described Seamus as 'the hardest going Golden' he had ever seen. Bryanstown Topaz, who won the Reserve CC at Cruft's, was one of the winners sired by Seamus.

A mating of Gale Warning's daughter Janacre Gaiety of Bryanstown to Ch. Stolford Happy Lad produced Bryanstown Solo and Bryanstown Modesty Blaise, who both won well. A repeat mating produced Ch. Bryanstown Gaucho. A Junior-Warrant winner, he won his title, eighteen CCs, fourteen Reserve CCs and was Best of Breed at Cruft's in 1981. Gaucho was worked regularly but was so accident-prone that he was retired early. He sired numerous winners including Sh.Ch. Linchael Excelsior. Oriole Drummer Boy is a Gaucho son who excelled in the field, where he had gained thirty field-trial awards. He is also a Championship Show winner.

The Bryanstown affix is now held by the Twists' daughter and son-in-law, Mr and Mrs Ewings. All the present-day dogs are decendants of Gale Warning and Gaucho, and all win and work.

The Lilling kennel started in 1948 when June Wood bought in two bitches. Mimosa of Lilling (by Torrdale Don Juan, ex Torrdale Jilly Flower) was bred by Mr Walker. The second, Timberscombe Crystal (by Ch. Dorcas Glorious of Slat, ex Timberscombe Trefoil) was bred by Mrs Cousins. Both won well and then Mrs Wood purchased a dog puppy. He was by Ch. Torrdale Happy Lad, ex Torrdale Chenilles Marigold and became Ch. Torrdale Faithful.

Although lightly shown, Freesia of Lilling won CCs as did Prince William of Lilling and Golden Shoes of Lilling. Faithful and Freesia qualified at field trials. Fiona of Lilling and Fanfare of Lilling were exported to Finland where they became champions and also qualified in the field. Laughter of Lilling went to India and Golden Eagle of Lilling went to Belgium.

In the 1940s and 1950s, most Golden Retrievers who were shown were also worked. Mrs Wood would like to see the return of Golden Retrievers needing to qualify at a field trial as she believes many have lost the instinct to work.

*Mrs June Wood with left to right: Torrbury Rosamund, Mimosa of
Lilling, Dream Boy of Lilling, Magnolia of Lilling, Crusader of
Lilling (hiding!), Boltby Spotlight, Ch. Torrdale Faithful (at back), and
Clover of Lilling. Photograph taken in 1954.*

Wendy and David Andrews founded their Catcombe kennel on
Ch. Royal Pal of Catcombe, who was bought in 1968 as a pet for the
family. She was sold cheaply as she 'was not of show quality'! In
1971, Honey was mated to Pennard Golden Brumas and his owner,
Mrs Thompson, persuaded Mr and Mrs Andrews to show her.
Honey's career began at an Exemption Show, when she was six
weeks in whelp. Ferelith Hamilton awarded her several firsts.

Encouraged by early success, Honey progressed to Championship
Shows, from where she never looked back. She won her first CC at
six and a half years and continued to win until she was nine and a half
years, when she won the CC at Cruft's, the CC and Best in Show at
the Golden Retreiver Club of Scotland and also the CC at the Golden
Retriever Club Show. Her eventual total was eleven CCs, six Best of
Breed awards, three Reserve CCs and a Gundog Group.

From Honey's litter to Pennard Golden Brumas, a bitch was kept:
Amber Charm of Catcombe. She emulated her dam's success by
gaining her title, winning eight CCs and four Reserve CCs. She also

Ch. Royal Pal of Catcombe, from pet to top winner, with 11 CCs to her credit. She was also a Group winner.

won Best of Breed at Cruft's in 1982. Charm had one litter to Catcombe Cupid, which produced the Open Stake field-trial winner, Catcombe Cabriole.

Ch. Royal Pal of Catcombe produced a litter to Raynesgold Rainaway and three puppies were retained: Catcombe Crystal won one CC but never produced puppies; Catcombe Ceraphim, who was never shown but was the first dog trained by Mr and Mrs Andrews; Catcombe Cherabin, was also worked and produced some excellent puppies. She is the dam of Cupid and Sericious by Sh.Ch. Concord of Yeo and of Chamois by Sh.Ch. Teecon Knighterrant.

The working side became increasingly important and enjoyable to Mr and Mrs Andrews, more so because the dogs so obviously enjoyed it. The natural progression was to introduce line-bred working Golden Retrievers into the Catcombe strain.

In 1978, Sheersilk of Yeo was bought from Mrs Sawtell. Sheersilk is a daughter of FTCh. Holway Chanter out of Shotsilk of Yeo. She

FTCh. Standerwick Rumbustious of Catcombe.

had the required speed and style and her long list of wins in field trials and working tests is proof of her worth. She won ten firsts in Open tests, including the Arthebray Cup for the highest placed dog at the United Retriever Club's area final. She has won placings in field-trial classes at Championship Shows, won awards in Obedience and, most important, she is a field-trial winner.

In 1982, Standerwick Rumbustious of Catcombe was purchased. He gained his Field Trial Champion title when he was four years old, having already won a non-winner trial at two years old and was also second and third in Open Stakes when he was three years old. His good looks and sound construction have won him many placings at Championship Shows as well, so he is a true dual-purpose Golden Retriever. Understandably, Wendy and David Andrews are delighted with his success, as a good-looking Golden Retriever who is

232

capable of achieving the highest standard in the field is of prime importance to them. Their dream is to have a Golden Retriever capable of winning CCs and also an Open Qualifying Stake.

The Nortonwood kennel is owned by Madge and Ron Bradbury. Their interest in Golden Retrievers began in the mid-1950s when they kept males of Fordvale, Beauchasse and Penkori lines and competed in Obedience.

Attempts at breeding were thwarted as the first three bitches bought in were found to have hereditary cataract. A fresh start was made with two bitches from the late Doris Dawson. These were Destiny of Milo (by Ch. Sansue Camrose Phoenix, ex Sh.Ch. Amber of Milo) and her younger sister Nortonwood Fantasy of Milo. Each bitch produced a champion: Destiny, mated to Ch. Cabus Caruso, produced Sh.Ch. Nortonwood Canella; and Fantasy, mated to Ch. Camrose Cabus Christopher, produced Ch. Nortonwood Faunus. When Canella was mated to Ch. Davern Figaro, the result was Sh.Ch. Nortonwood Checkmate, who is known as a producer of good hips.

Faunus had an outstanding career, winning thirteen CCs, twenty-eight Reserve CCs, one Gundog Group and one Reserve in Group. As a sire, his success is legendary. He held the Golden Retriever Club's Stud-Dog Cup for eight consecutive years (a breed record). He sired eighteen British title-holders and more abroad, having a great influence on Golden Retrievers overseas. The mating of Faunus to Ch. Westley Victoria produced six champions, and to Ch. Styal Susila resulted in three champions. It is interesting to note that these were half-brother, half-sister matings.

Sh.Ch. Nortonwood Checkmate was bred to be mated to Faunus daughters and this proved a most successful combination producing Sh.Ch. Nortonwood Silvanus, Ch. Nortonwood Secreto (Sweden) and Ch. Nortonwood Squire (Australia). A Faunus × Checkmate combination produced the top-winning dog and bitch at the World Show in Denmark in 1989.

Other top-winning Golden Retrievers living at Nortonwood include Sh.Ch. Ninell Charade of Nortonwood, Sh.Ch. Westley Munro of Nortonwood, Westley Sabrina of Nortonwood (two CCs), Amirene Egretta of Nortonwood (two CCs), and Sh.Ch. Jobeka Jasper of Nortonwood. Ch. Nortonwood Marx was also bred by the Bradburys.

Mrs Hazel Hinks of the Styal kennel acquired her first Golden Retriever in 1951. This was Judy of Anbria (Julie) who was litter-sister to Ch. Jane of Anbria (dam of Ch. Camrose Tallyrand of Anbria). Julie's sire was Ch. William of Westley.

Two years later, the Hinks family moved to Jordan. Julie eventually arrived and she proved to be an excellent gundog. She was also very beautiful, being a glamorous blonde. Like most of her breed, she was excellent with children and everyone loved her. She was the only Golden Retriever in Jordan.

Owing to the family's extensive travelling, Julie was never mated. Two foundation bitches were chosen from the Camrose kennel. One, Camrose Wistara, was a great character but not a good brood-bitch. The other, Camrose Gilda proved to be an excellent brood if not a very good show bitch.

Gilda was mated to Ch. Camrose Nicolas of Westley, a lovely extrovert blonde dog. Gilda always looked very proud with a beautiful neck and shoulders and regal head carriage and appeared rather disdainful. In her first litter there were two lovely blonde bitches, a colour rather unusual then and not at all popular.

Marigold Timson loved them and when the mating was repeated she had the pick of the bitches: Styal Sonnet. Sonnet was mated to Ch. Camrose Cabus Christopher and this produced the gorgeous Pippa girls in Marigold's Sh.Ch. Gyrima Pipparetta, Heather Morris's Sh.Ch. Gyrima Pipparanda, and Vivien Jones' Ch. Gyrima Pippalina. These were the foundation bitches of the Sandusky and Ninell kennels.

Sibella became Mrs Hinks' first champion and although she had one of the most beautiful heads ever seen in the breed, great difficulty was encountered in making her up. Her colour was much disliked by many judges and she won ten Reserve CCs and just the three CCs required for her title. When she won Best Veteran Bitch at The Golden Retriever Club Championship Show, the dog judge, a very famous lady, was heard to remark, when deciding on Best Veteran in Show, 'The dog! I will not concede to *that* colour!'

Sibella and Sophia were both mated to Christopher and this combination proved very successful. Sibella produced two outstanding bitches, one of which was Ch. Styal Stephanie of Camrose, the bitch breed record-holder with twenty-seven CCs.

Ch. Styal Susila won ten CCs in a spectacular career spanning almost eleven years. She was six and a half months old when her career began and she was awarded Best Puppy in Show and also Best in Show by the late Arthur Westlake. At her last show, the Golden Retriever Club Championship Show, ten years later, she won the

*Ch. Styal Susila, a beautiful bitch of outstanding balance and
conformation. (Photo Pearce)*

Reserve CC and Best Veteran in Show. Earlier in her career she was a
finalist in the Pup of the Year competition and, whilst she was
competing, her sister Stephanie was winning the Reserve CC. They
were just nine months old.

Susila was a natural worker and won a novice dog/handler test at
eight and a half months old. She was an outstanding brood-bitch and
over a period of six years she was three times Top Brood-Bitch and
three times the runner-up to the great Ch. Westley Victoria.

Susila was the dam of Sh.Ch. Styal Symetrya (ten CCs) and her
most successful mating was to Ch. Nortonwood Faunus, which
produced the outstanding Poets litter, Sh.Ch. Styal Shelley of
Maundale, Sh.Ch. Styal Shakespeare and the great Ch. Styal Scott
of Glengilde, the breed record-holder with forty-two CCs.

Golden Retrievers from the Styal kennel have been very success-
ful abroad with five international champions and four champions.
The Sophia/Christopher mating produced Nor. Ch. Styal Schimiter,
Swiss Ch. Styal Serriff and Singapore Ch. Styal Sophieson. Ch.
Styal Susila was the dam of Nor. Ch. Styal Schimeon and Sp. Ch.

Ch. Styal Sibella,
illustrating her beautiful head
and expression. (Photo Pearce)

Styal Sascilia who was full sister to the Poets and Styal Solacea.

The mating of Styal Solacea to Sh.Ch. Nortonwood Checkmate was another extremely successful combination, producing Int. Ch. and Swiss Ch. Styal Samourai, Int. Ch. and Bel. Ch. Styal Sungleam and Int. Ch. and Ger. Ch. Styal Solar. All three have won well in the field. Two recent champions abroad are Int. Ch. Styal Stargleam in Germany, and Swiss Ch. Styal Snowstorm.

Mrs Hinks usually keeps just four or five bitches and all are much loved house pets and accompany her at all times. For this reason, numbers have always consciously been kept low. She regards the keeping of Golden Retrievers as 'a wonderful, rewarding hobby' and is grateful for the many friends it has brought her from varied walks of life throughout the world.

Appendix 1

Golden Retriever Clubs in the UK

The Golden Retriever Club
Mrs T. Theed,
Squirrelsmead Cottage
Fivehead
Taunton
Somerset TA3 6QY

Golden Retriever Club of
Scotland
Mr E. Fogg
7 Pitcullen Terrace
Perth PH2 7EQ

All-Ireland Golden Retriever
Club
Mrs T. Molony
The Green
Holycross
Co. Tipperary

Golden Retriever Club of
Wales
Mr A. Fall
3 Curlew Close
Rest Bay, Porthcawl
Mid Glamorgan

Ulster Golden Retriever Club
Mrs M. Neill
'Alma Rosa'
49 Brackagh Mos Road
Portadown, Craigavon
Northern Ireland

Southern Golden Retriever
Society
Miss G. Clark
Stocks Green Cottage
Ring's Hill
Hildenborough
Nr. Tonbridge
Kent

North West Golden Retriever
Club
Mrs J. Robinson
Jojander
32 Meadowcroft
Euxton, Chorley
Lancs PR7 6BU

Golden Retriever Club of
Northumbria
Mrs J. Hay
12 Hedley Road
Holywell, Whitley Bay
Tyne & Wear NE25 0NW

Northern Golden Retriever
Association
Mrs U. Spratt
Cliff Cottage
Lincoln Road
Boothby Graffoe
Lincoln LN5 0LB

Midland Golden Retriever
Club
Mr R. Hibbs
8 Overdale Road
New Mills
Nr. Stockport
Cheshire SK12 3LJ

Eastern Counties Golden
Retriever Club
Mrs B. Webb
116 Cambridge Road
Great Shelford
Cambridgeshire CB2 5JS

Berkshire Downs & Chilterns
Golden Retriever Club
Mr P. R. Cullen
Aynho Park Lodge
Aynho
Banbury
Oxon

South Western Golden
Retriever Club
Mr R. Coward
'Green Acres'
Ibsley Drove
Ibsley
Nr Ringwood
Hampshire
BH24 3NP

Yorkshire Golden Retriever
Club
Miss D. Frazer
Shamanda Cottage
2 Tateley Lane
Ossett
West Yorkshire

Appendix 2

Golden Retriever Clubs in the USA

GRC of Greater Los Angeles
Linda Hurd
4954 Alta Canyada Road
LA Canada
CA 91011

GRC of San Diego County
Linda McIntyre
12942 Francine Terrace
Poway
CA 92064

Nor-Cal GRC
Nancy Hopkins
1551 Solitude Lane
Elsobrante
CA 94083

Atlanta GRC
Bob Campbell
7000 Yachting Way
Acworth
GA 30101

GRC of Hawaii
Twylla Dawn Steer
618 Paopua Loop
Kailua
HI 96734

Des Moines GRC
Charlene Wilson
RTI Cumming
IA 50061

APPENDICES

GRC of Illinois
Jerry Stecker
914 Fair Oaks
Deerfield
IL 60015

Kansas City GRC
Sarah E. Karl
1408 North 81st Street
Kansas City
KS 66112

Yankee GRC
Judith Suket
76 Bicknell Street
Quincy ,
MA 02169

Ford Detroit GRC
Irene Young
30571 Wentworth
Livonia
MI 48154

Greater Twin Cities GRC
Mary Ellen M. Otis
2447 W. County Road B
Apt 9
St Paul
MN 55113

Triad GRC
Karen McClung
7321 Horseman's Cove
Kernersville
NC 27284

Garden State GRC
Judy Laureano
14 Cross Street
Allsdale
NJ 07642

Lenape GRC
S. Hope Meaker
PO Box 464
Milford
NI 088481

GRC of Western New York
Earlene Kettle
7988 Lewiston Road
Batavia
NY 14020

Hudson Valley GRC
Juliet Mastrangelo
3 Clover Road
Valhalla
NY 10595

Long Island GRC
Jeff Sievers
PO Box 59
Calverton
NY 11933

Cuyahoga Valley GRC
Nancy Lanigan
2240 Briarwood Road
Cleveland Heights
OH 44118

Greater Cincinnati GRC
Terri Kocher
33 Schneider Drive
Fairborn
OH 45324

Central Oklahoma GRC
Debi
4003 Lawn Drive
Del City
OK 73115

Greater Tulsa GRC
Julia Strong
4150 South Cincinnati
Tulsa
OK 74105

Greater Pittsburgh GRC
Martha J. Cromer
5217 Glenwall Drive
Aliquippa
PA 15001

Austin GRC
Roger Fuller
3705 Peach Vista
Plugeville
TX 78660

Dallas-Fort Worth Metro GRC
Cathie Newitt
124 Woodhaven Court
Red Oak
TX 75154

Greater Houston GRC
Patti Layne
6606 Vickie Springs
Houston
TX 77086

Potomac Valley GRC
Don T. Wilson
6558 Marlo Drive
Falls Church
VA 22042

Evergreen GRC
Jennifer Gabriel
14511 Wallingford Avenue
North Seattle
WA 98133

Badger GRC
Joan Kaml
4480 North 144 Street
Brookfield
WI 53005

Appendix 3

BVA/Kennel Club Approved Ophthalmologists

Certificates of freedom from hereditary eye defects are only obtainable from the following panel of examiners, who are ophthalmologists approved by the British Veterinary Association /Kennel Club (BVA /KC) Eye Scheme.

England
K.W. Barber, BVetMed,
  MRCVS
97 Mount Pleasant
Redditch
Hereford and Worcester

Dr K.C. Barnett, MA, BSc,
  FRCVS
The Animal Health Trust
Small Animals Centre
Lanwades Park
Kennett, Newmarket
Suffolk CB8 7PN

M.T. Bate, BVMS, MRCVS
87 Watford Road
Cotteridge
Birmingham B30 1NP

APPENDICES

Dr P.G.C. Bedford, BVetMed,
  FRCVS (chief panellist)
Royal Veterinary College
Hawkshead House
Hawkshead Lane
North Mymms, Hatfield
Hertfordshire AL9 7TA

N.J. Burden, BVSc, MRCVS
19 Langley Road
Chippenham
Wiltshire SN15 1BS

Dr S.M. Crispin, MA, BSc,
  VetMB, MRCVS
Dept of Veterinary Surgery
University of Bristol
Langford House
Langford
Bristol BS18 7DU

Dr R. Curtis, MSc, BVSc,
  DTVM, MRCVS
The Animal Health Trust
Small Animals Centre
Lanwades Park
Kennett, Newmarket
Suffolk CB8 7PN

J.B. Errington, BVMS,
  MRCVS
19 Ayres Terrace
North Shields
Tyne and Wear

P.J. Evans, VetMB, MRCVS
Moreton Eye
Leominster
Hereford and Worcester
HR6 0DP

S.J. Foster, BVSc, MRCVS
The Veterinary Hospital
34 Dover Road
Canterbury
Kent CT1 3DT

J.V. Goodyear, BVMS,
  MRCVS
90 Spring Terrace Road
Burton on Trent
Staffordshire

J.S. Heath, MRCVS
The 608 Veterinary Group
608 Warwick Road
Solihull
West Midlands

D.M. Heeley, MRCVS
Brooksden Veterinary Hospital
Cranbrook
Kent TN17 3DS

D.G. Knight, MRCVS
177 Kirkstall Lane
Leeds 6

M.P.C. Lawton, BVetMed,
  MRCVS
12 Fitzilian Avenue
Harold Wood, Romford
Essex RM3 0QS

A. Leon, BVMS, MRCVS
The Animal Health Trust
Small Animals Centre
Lanwades Park
Kennett, Newmarket
Suffolk CB8 7PN

D.G. Lewis, FRCVS, DVR
  University of Liverpool
Veterinary Hospital
Crown Street
Liverpool L7 7EX

S.J. Lewis, BVSc, MRCVS
The Rokery
Yoxall
Burton-on-Trent
Staffordshire DE13 8NH

R.D. Long, BVetMed, MRCVS
41 High Street
Wimbledon Common
London SW19 5AU

J.K. Mason, MA, VetMB,
  MRCVS
Seadown Veterinary Hospital
Frost Lane
Hythe
Southampton SO4 6NG

S.M. Petersen-Jones,
  BVetMed, MRCVS
Royal Veterinary College
Hawkshead House
Hawkshead Lane
North Mymms, Hatfield
Hertfordshire AL9 7TA

J.D. Ricketts, BVMS, MRCVS
Royd Cottage
38 Sude Hill
New Mill, Huddersfield
West Yorkshire HD7 7BZ

Miss J. Sansom, BVSc,
  MRCVS
University of Liverpool
Veterinary Hospital
Crown Street
Liverpool L7 7EX

Dr F.G. Startup, BSc, FRCVS
West Mount
Hambrook Hill
Chichester
Sussex PO18 8UQ

C.G.B. Warren, BA, VetMB,
  MRCVS
1 Whitchurch Road
Tavistock
Devon

Channel Islands
J.J. Yelowley, BVSc, MRCVS
Sommet Vert Veterinary
  Surgery
Route de Genets
St. Brelade
Jersey
Channel Islands

Scotland
M.G. Davidson, BVMS,
  MRCVS
19 Hillhouse Road
Edinburgh 4

Professor D.D. Lawson, PhD,
  BSc, MRCVS, DVR
Burn Brae
Balfoen
Glasgow G63 0NY

Professor J.S.A. Spreull,
  PhD, MRCVS, DVR
Spencerfield House
Hillend
Dunfermline
Fife

A.E. Wall, BVMS, MRCVS
The Veterinary Surgery
Rogard
Highland

Wales
Mrs G.E. Hubbard, BVetMed,
  MRCVS
Bryn Eisteddfod
South Street
Caernarvon
Gwynedd

H.R. Williams, BVSc, MRCVS
Moat Village Farm
New Moat
Clarbeston Road
Dyfed SA3 4RH

Northern Ireland
W.D.J. McCartney, BSc,
  MRCVS
Cedar Grove
Upper Knockbreda Road
Belfast BT6 9QB

I. Millar, BVMS, MRCVS
Earlswood Veterinary Hospital
193 Belmont Road
Belfast

Eire
Dr T.D. Grimes, BVetMed,
  DVR
University of Dublin
Faculty of Veterinary Medicine
Veterinary College of Ireland
Ballsbridge
Dublin 4

Index